For Xôi.

You have filled my heart with more love than I ever realized it could hold. At a time of global isolation you made our little world feel closer and more connected than ever. Because of you, I finally found the me I'd been searching for. So proud to be your mummy!

Always.

VIETNAMESE

Thuy Diem Pham

SIMPLE, MODERN RECIPES FOR EVERY DAY

cover illustration by Jordan Amy Lee
photography by Laura Edwards

MADE EASY

Hardie Grant

QUADRILLE

Introduction

We've all experienced those moments when you suddenly question something quite fundamental to you. A moment when you realize that maybe you've actually had it wrong all along. At the time it felt like a harsh awakening: expecting my first child, at such an uncertain time for the whole world, helped me to see things from a completely different perspective, which is rarely a bad thing. More importantly, it was the start of a journey that took me from staunch traditionalist, insisting the only way to cook 'authentically' was to spend many hours toiling away in the kitchen, all the way here to *Vietnamese Made Easy*.

To understand why it was such a sea change for me I'll briefly head back to November 1981, when a hungry little girl was born to two loving parents in a small village called Hanh My in the south of Vietnam, in among the beautiful rivers of the Mekong Delta. In the aftermath of the war, things were very different: food became scarce and life was extremely difficult for the whole region. To supplement milk, mum would often feed my sister and I the starchy water left over from cooking rice. With hindsight it is obvious that given the diet my mum had at the time, there probably wasn't much milk in the first place, especially with the number of meals she would skip just so that we could eat. Now more than ever, I appreciate the sacrifices she made for us. I used to think I understood what was meant by the phrase 'a mother's love', but as clichéd as it is to say, a whole new world opened up for me when my son was born and I finally realized that it wasn't just hyperbole.

Growing up, every meal was precious. Always humble, yet always delicious. The effort put in by the women of the family at mealtimes was immense. For celebrations and holidays this would be even more evident as all the aunties would gather to help prepare the 'feast' for the day. So much so that I always felt the real party was in the kitchen. It was the loudest room by far, with constant stories, gossip and laughter alongside the wonderfully enticing bubbling and hissing of cooking food. Music to my ears from as far back as I can remember and, to this day, something that is guaranteed to start my belly rumbling, regardless of the time of day. The only thing more tantalizing were the aromas of the broths and the spices that would escape from the kitchen, lingering and teasing everyone in the house. Being the hungry and impatient child that I was, I worked hard to find the perfect balance of persistent and cute to ensure that when quality control was needed, I was first in line for a cheeky taster from grandma, the head chef of this wonderful chaos.

In the summer of 1989, I stepped off the plane at London's Heathrow airport, one hand tightly holding on to mum's while the other clung to a little wooden box. A present for my dad that I'd held all the way from Vietnam. When we left it had been full of his favourite fruit, longan, which back then was impossible to buy in the UK. I remember being a bit nervous giving it to him, partly because he'd left Vietnam when I was just three so I had no real memory of him and only even knew what he looked like thanks to a couple of battered photographs, but mainly because the box was empty. The airline food really hadn't looked appetizing to me and I had once again let my hunger get the better of me. According to the family stories I had insisted on bringing the fruit for Dad and, despite the fact that I'd eaten it long before it had got to him, I was more than happy to describe what the gift had been and go into great detail about how delicious and succulent it had tasted. My family love to remind me of this story as another example of how much I love my food.

Looking back through adult eyes I think that it's clear that I was clutching on to that little empty box of longan, as it felt like I had a small piece of home with me, on what must have been a very scary day for a seven year old. In a way, this is a metaphor for what I have continued to do with Vietnamese food since, both through my work as a chef and with my family whenever we gather together. I believe that this has helped to keep my memories of Vietnam alive over all these years. Thirty odd years on and I can still close my eyes and step back into grandma's kitchen like it was yesterday. Every recipe handed down has been treasured and passed on with a sense of reverence. Of course each generation adds its own tweak or twist here and there, but always with a fundamental level of respect to the recipe. I was taught to value the traditional techniques and to take a genuine pride in my cooking – to embrace and appreciate the ingredients we had in order to maximize and enhance the flavours, helping to turn the humblest ingredients into incredible dishes. Food is the not-so-hidden language of familial love in Vietnam, passed down generation upon generation, so it comes as no surprise that traditional and 'authentic' Vietnamese recipes are considered sacrosanct.

As I grew older I came to realize that these recipes can vary greatly by region, village and even household. Each family having their own exact set of rules. It is only when you start to build up a much larger picture of lots of these different sets of rules that you start to notice the overarching patterns and themes that make up Vietnamese cuisine: freshness of ingredients, punchy flavours and, most of all, intricately balanced tastes and textures.

As with the majority of Vietnam's cooks and chefs, I was inspired and trained by my mum. I was also fortunate enough to be surrounded by my grandma and lots of aunties, all happy to share their many years of experience with me. So I approached my new career as a chef with my own restaurant – The Little Viet Kitchen – as confident as a graduate straight from Le Cordon Bleu. I can still vividly remember our first service and the very rude awakening that came with it! But never being one to turn down a challenge, I rolled up the sleeves on my new chef jacket and went again the next day.

The Little Viet Kitchen soon became a much-loved dining venue for locals as well as people from all across the globe, some who would travel thousands of miles to eat our food. Something that never failed to amaze, humble and delight us, in equal measure.

My key takeaway from those years running LVK is practice, practice, practice! Very few recipes turn out perfectly the first time you try, and actually the fun is in the development. The hours spent experimenting with recipes and techniques are some of the happiest of my life. Nothing quite beats the moment when you absolutely nail a dish. The sense of achievement and pride when the empty plates start making their way back to the kitchen is what it was all about. Even now it makes me smile when I see a short rib served on Phở knowing that my creation is still making people happy all over the world.

A pandemic and a beautiful baby boy later and it's fair to say that my world has changed quite dramatically. It turns out that there is nothing quite like long queues for empty supermarket shelves to bring you back to the fundamentals of cooking. The challenge had gone full circle and once again became about making the best of what I had. I embraced my new normal and set about re-creating familiar flavours and textures, noting down interesting combinations and little newfound tricks and hacks.

This quickly became my new passion and soon the concept for *Vietnamese Made Easy* was born. The objective was simple: to use my understanding of the essence of Vietnamese cuisine combined with my professional experience to create amazing, achievable dishes at home. Every meal should be special regardless of how much time you have to prepare it.

Vietnamese food is essentially about contrast and balance. Each dish should be a balance of different elements like sweet and salty, with contrasts of texture and temperature, as well as flavour. It does not need to be complicated, just balanced and tasty!

The aim of this book is to showcase a different side to Vietnamese cookery, one that can be quick, accessible, delicious and nourishing.

As a new mum, I have realized that sometimes shortcuts are necessary and that there is a place for quick-to-the-table delicious food in modern family life, with a few ingredient swaps here and there. Our increasingly busy lives mean we're giving ourselves less time to cook than ever before, and when we do, it's often a choice between convenience and nutrition. But it really doesn't have to be. These recipes are as balanced as they are delicious, while being stress-free and simple to prepare. Depending on where you live, traditional Vietnamese ingredients can be hard to find, so where possible I have switched to easy-to-source alternatives.

You'll find that the recipes throughout this book are varied and versatile; they're influenced by my childhood in Vietnam, but also by my current life with my family in London, so you'll find a mix of recipes – some traditional with twists, some new favourites that bring together Vietnamese flavours with other international influences, all created with respect and love.

Today my boy will often be found happily on my hip, while I cook our family meal with the other hand. Despite the extra effort, I love that he enjoys being in the kitchen with me. Even though my little sous chef is only a year old as I write this, he is already fascinated by all the sounds of cooking and is constantly investigating the different ingredients. He's never afraid of trying a new flavour. I can't wait to teach him all I know, just like my mum did for me. Luckily for him, as you will find when you turn the page, rather than sticking with the traditional 'bit of this, bit of that' mum approach, I am actually writing the recipes down.

Using this book: Shopping essentials

Here is a handy shopping list featuring a few essentials that appear often throughout this book. Take special note of the fresh ingredients here, as the key to the beautiful, aromatic Vietnamese flavours is in the fresh herbs. To my mind, you can never have too many fresh ingredients, so experiment with the different flavours and add something a little extra to your bowl.

USEFUL FRESH INGREDIENTS

- **Fresh lime juice** helps to balance out a dish. The sour notes balance out the fish or soy sauce, and the acidity helps to cut through the spice of chillies and ginger. Bottled can be used as an alternative to fresh, although it isn't as good.

- **Spring onions (scallions) and chives** are mostly used as garnishes. They have a fresh spicy kick, a slightly crunchy texture and a beautiful deep green colour for presentation.

- **Red (Asian) shallots** are a touch sweeter than the British variety, so are preferred in Vietnamese cooking. Shallots are used both to add an extra layer of sweetness to a dish and as a crunchy garnish.

- **Coriander (cilantro)** is used extensively throughout Vietnamese cuisine as it adds wonderful fragrance, freshness and flavour that help to elevate a meal.

- **Thai basil** looks beautiful as a garnish and packs a fiercely delicious aniseed punch that adds another dimension to your dish. Italian basil is very different and shouldn't be substituted.

- **Vietnamese mint** isn't botanically related to British mint, but can generally be used interchangeably as a garnish. While the taste is quite different, it brings a similar fragrance and a fresh, slightly spicy kick to the bite.

While fresh is always ideal, the following ingredients can be substituted with a jarred paste without compromising the dish too much:

- **Lemongrass** is present in almost every Vietnamese dish and, due to its delicious sweet citrus flavour, is perfect for adding a zest to your sauce or marinade.

- **Ginger** is a key spice in any Vietnamese larder, used to add a warm, spicy and comforting flavour to your dish.

- **Garlic** is another ever-present ingredient in Vietnamese cuisine, used as a base flavour ingredient in most stocks, marinades and sauces.

- **Red chillies** are essential for adding a little heat to your dish. In Vietnam, the chilli of choice is usually bird's-eye.

USEFUL LARDER INGREDIENTS

Larder ingredients provide a lot of flavour and balance to a recipe. Using good-quality items will go a long way to making a winning dish and here I've listed some of my favourites.

- **Fish sauce** is the staple of every Vietnamese larder, used to add salt and umami to most Vietnamese dishes. Fish sauce also has a slight sour note to it that should be considered when balancing a dish, which is why you often find salt alongside it as an ingredient in a recipe. I regularly use Squid, a Thai brand of fish sauce, or the Vietnamese brand Son, if I can get hold of it.

- **Light and dark soy sauce** can be a little confusing, as light soy is actually the punchier of the two. Dark soy is less salty than its counterpart and is used to give a depth of colour rather than taste. Often a recipe will call for both varieties to maximize colour, as well as flavour. Amoy is a great brand.

- **Honey** is used as a substitute for sugar as a sweetener in marinades and sauces when a more floral or fruity note is preferred.

- **Tamarind paste** is an absolute flavour bomb of an ingredient! Only a small amount is needed to create huge sweet and sour flavours. Perfect to liven up any salad or stir-fry.

- **Oyster sauce** adds a delicious meaty flavour and a heavy thickness to a sauce. Essentially it does a similar job to soy, but with an added depth of umami. I use Amoy.

- **Chicken bouillon, or chicken stock cubes**, are a quick and convenient way to instantly add a deep flavour base to your dish. Knorr is one of my favourite brands. True Foods also make delicious stock.

- **Sweet chilli sauce** is an instant way to add sweet, sour, salty and spicy flavours while also adding thickness to your sauce.

- **Rice wine vinegar** can be used as a substitute for lime juice. I prefer to use lime where possible as it brings a lovely freshness to a dish, but rice wine vinegar can be stored for years so is a very handy alternative.

- **Black pepper** is a must-have ingredient; it adds the perfect level of light spicy taste by itself, but also works very well in tandem with chilli and ginger to add that wonderful layering of spice to a dish.

- **Shrimp paste** is the ultimate umami ingredient, adding a deep flavour and aromatic fragrance to a finished dish. You'll find this in Vietnamese supermarkets or online. Alternatively, you can use 'umami paste', which is often available in supermarkets.

- **Cornflour (cornstarch)** is a thickening agent that adds density to a sauce. This helps to better coat the food, adding more flavour to the bite.

- **Vegetable oil** is my preferred cooking oil, as it is subtle in taste, so does the job required without flavouring the dish.

- **Sesame oil** comes into its own as an ingredient rather than a cooking oil, as it brings a deliciously rich, nutty flavour. It is great to use as a seasoning and perfect in a marinade to tenderize meat. I like to use Amoy's sesame oil.

NOODLES AND RICE

- **Phở** are flat rice noodles used almost exclusively in Phở broths. However, they can also add a delicious variation of texture to a stir-fry. Lucky Boat is my favourite brand.

- **Udon** are thick wheat noodles that are excellent for stir-fries as they retain their bouncy, firm texture through the cooking process and absorb maximum levels of flavour. While they are not traditionally used in Vietnamese cuisine, I have used them in this book to replace bánh canh, a tapioca noodle with a similar texture that is predominantly eaten with broths in Vietnam.

- **Vermicelli** are the most commonly used noodles in Vietnamese cuisine. These thin rice noodles are a lighter option, yet still absorb flavours well. Delicious hot or cold, they are perfect for broths, salads or rolls. I like Lucky Boat's, if I can get hold of them.

- **Jasmine rice** is eaten in some form with almost every meal in Vietnam. The variant is grown extensively in the country and is available in abundance. It is soft, fluffy and a little sticky, although a lot less so than sticky or glutinous rice.

- **Sticky rice** is a type of rice that in Vietnam is used mainly for desserts or special occasions, due to being naturally sweeter and a little more expensive than jasmine rice.

UTENSILS

- A **bamboo steamer** is a simple yet essential kitchen tool that dates back thousands of years. If you don't have a steamer, take your largest saucepan with a lid, or a small stockpot, and place a bowl upside down on the bottom. Fill the pan with water to just below the top of the bowl, then place a second bowl, the correct way up, securely on top of the first. Put the lid on and you have a working steamer!

- **Electric rice cookers** are commonplace in Vietnamese households as they are cheap, simple to use and produce perfect rice every time; they are so much more effective than a saucepan. The recipes in this book do not require a rice cooker, but they do make life easier.

- Often referred to as an infuser, a **spice strainer** is simply a mesh ball used to hold spices without them escaping into the broth. If you don't have one large enough for the volume of spice required then you can substitute with a tightly tied piece of muslin (cheesecloth).

- A **mesh strainer** is an invaluable tool for achieving a clear soup, as it can be used to gently remove impurities without overly disturbing the broth.

- A **pestle and mortar** is a handy kitchen staple for grinding and mixing ingredients.

- A little trick to know when your oil is ready to start cooking is to place a **wooden chopstick** in the oil, and when bubbles start forming around it, your oil is ready to go.

BROTHS & SOUPS

Feed the Soul

Broths and noodle soups are the heart-warming soul of Vietnamese cuisine; for generations, the Vietnamese have cooked these dishes with pride and served them with love. It is no secret that us Viets take it as a personal affront when we see our national dish, Phở, being made in a non-traditional way. It has long been agreed that many hours of laborious processes are essential in order to create the perfectly balanced bowl of broth. And I know I speak for most when I say that in that moment when it's just you and your bowl of noodles it's pure bliss! Phở has long been held up as the pinnacle of Vietnamese cuisine, made famous outside the country thanks to its popularity with tourists – partly because it's served throughout every region of the country and partly, of course, because it's simply very tasty. However, Vietnam has so many more broths to enjoy that are just as wonderful. In this chapter I will share and showcase some of those, and along the way throw in a couple of my own creations, too.

When cooking Vietnamese, there are many clear rules in place to preserve the sanctity of traditional recipes, although I have found those rules often vary greatly from region to region, even house to house, while remaining unfailingly absolute in their dogma. I have been brought up this way as well to always be mindful of the recipe passed down from as far back as anyone in the family can remember. My first cookbook, *The Little Viet Kitchen*, has several of these recipes that need five to ten hours before that perfect bowl is served. I wrote each one to my own family's rulebook, whole-heartedly and respectfully.

However, what I'm about to share with you in this chapter can be seen as game-changing if, like me, you don't have eight hours to prepare dinner, yet still want something homely, healthy and delicious. Or bordering on blasphemous if you are of my grandma's generation.

This chapter sidesteps and shortcuts several of the most time-consuming elements of Vietnamese broth building, instead focusing on the gorgeous toppings. The aim is to allow you to concentrate on creating your perfect flavours using amazing fresh ingredients. I should add that while placing less reliance on the broth, rest assured that we will by no means ignore the importance of it. Instead, my aim is simply to employ the odd trick here and there to create those rich aromatics without having to put in the hours.

I hope these pages bring you as much joy as they have to my family and me. My intention is never to replace the traditional, rather to provide an alternative for when a hectic life doesn't allow the luxury of time. Whether you are working full time or just busy trying to be the best parent you can be, these recipes will allow you to spend less time cooking and more time eating, and that can never be a bad thing!

Aromatic Beef Noodle Soup

SERVES 4

COOKING TIME: 1 HOUR 10 MINUTES

300g (10½oz) Phở rice noodles

100g (3½oz) beansprouts

500g (1lb 2oz) beef topside (top round)

4 beef marrow halves, 10–12cm (4–5in) long, halved lengthways

1 large red onion, thinly sliced lengthways

FOR THE BROTH

10 shallots (or 2 medium onions), peeled and halved

100g (3½oz) fresh ginger, halved and crushed (skin on)

5g (⅕oz) cinnamon stick

1 tsp coriander seeds

3 black cardamom pods

3 cloves

10 star anise

2 litres (4¼ pints) beef stock

500ml (17fl oz/generous 2 cups) chicken stock

500–600g (1lb 2oz–1lb 5oz) daikon (mooli), peeled and halved (or swede)

3 chicken stock cubes, crumbled

3 tsp salt

5 tsp sugar

5 tsp fish sauce

3 tsp beef dripping or vegetable oil

Phở is the pride and joy of Vietnamese culture. It's the flag bearer for our cuisine internationally and for good reason; it exquisitely showcases the intricate techniques and the depth and subtlety of flavour that our food embodies.

Similarly to other popular noodle soup dishes, these days I mostly hear people saying that they only make it on special occasions, as it's just too time intensive. While this is understandable, I still feel that it's worth doing when you do have the time. But for those days when you don't, I have created this recipe for you to enjoy those amazing flavours in a fraction of the time, reducing the 8 hours down to just over one!

My hope is that you will enjoy this simplified recipe so much that you'll seek out my traditional recipe and give that a go, too. In the meantime, let's get this beef noodle soup cooking!

I have added a 'feeling fancy' option that includes adding my signature coconut braised beef short rib, which is by no means traditional, but it's a delicious addition. It admittedly needs a few hours of braising but it's mainly the oven doing the work, so, if you have time, it's worth it.

For the broth, char the peeled shallots and ginger (with skin on) until brown and set aside.

Meanwhile, put the cinnamon, coriander seeds, cardamom, cloves and star anise into a dry pan and toast for 4–5 minutes over a medium heat, keeping it moving throughout to avoid burning. Add to a large tea/spice strainer (or tie up in a muslin/cheesecloth pouch) and set aside.

Cook the noodles according to the packet instructions, then drain and set aside.

Put the beansprouts into a heatproof bowl, add boiling water to cover, leave for a few seconds, then drain and set aside to dry.

Preheat the oven temperature to 220°C/430°F/ Gas 7.

RECIPE CONTINUES

FOR THE GARNISH

4 spring onions (scallions),
  finely chopped

20g (¾oz) Thai basil, leaves picked

10g (⅓oz) coriander (cilantro),
  finely chopped

2 red chillies, thinly sliced

2 tbsp crispy fried shallots
  (store-bought or see page 184)

1 lime, cut into 8 wedges

4 tbsp hoisin sauce

4 tbsp sriracha chilli sauce

FEELING FANCY OPTION

4 beef short ribs, each about
  250g (9oz)

1 tsp salt

2 tsp vegetable oil

1.5 litres (3¼ pints) coconut water

2 tsp fish sauce

2 tsp sugar

5 star anise

2 lemongrass stalks, crushed

2 garlic cloves

5g (⅕oz) fresh ginger, peeled

Cut the beef lengthways into 4 strips, then slice across the strips as thinly as possible. It is important that the meat is sliced very thinly so that it cooks when the broth is poured over, otherwise it will be chewy. If you have time, a tip here is to wrap the strips in clingfilm (plastic wrap) and put in the freezer for 30 minutes. This makes precision slicing so much easier!

Add the beef and chicken stocks and 500ml (17fl oz/generous 2 cups) water to a large saucepan or stockpot and bring to the boil over a high heat. Add the daikon, spice strainer or muslin of toasted spices, charred shallots and ginger. Add the remaining broth ingredients and reduce to a simmer for 30 minutes.

Roast the bone marrow in the oven for 20–25 minutes until slightly browned.

Return to the broth and, using a mesh strainer, remove all the solids, leaving just the broth. Skim any impurities off the top of the broth, if there are any, and then leave to simmer for 5 minutes while you serve.

Place the noodles in your serving bowls and top with the beansprouts, red onion and slices of raw beef. Pour the hot broth directly onto the beef so it cooks as it's served. Finally, scoop the bone marrow into your bowl and stir it into the broth.

Garnish with the spring onions (scallions), Thai basil, coriander (cilantro) and chilli, and sprinkle over some crispy fried shallots. Then serve with a lime wedge and small bowls of hoisin and sriracha for dipping.

FEELING FANCY OPTION
Preheat the oven to 180°C/350°F/Gas 4.

Lightly rub the ribs with the salt.

Add the oil to an ovenproof casserole dish and place over a high heat. Once hot, add the ribs and sear evenly for about 1 minute on each side.

Add all the ingredients to the casserole dish, cover and bake in the oven for 2½ hours, then serve with your Phở. You could cook the ribs the day before and then simply heat it up when serving.

Bún Gà Huế

SERVES 4

COOKING TIME: 1 HOUR
10 MINUTES

2 tsp vegetable oil

10 shallots (or 2 medium onions),
peeled and halved

100g (3½oz) fresh ginger, halved
and crushed

6 lemongrass stalks, crushed

½ fresh pineapple, peeled
and quartered

10 star anise

1 tsp coriander seeds

400g (14oz) vermicelli rice noodles

100g (3½oz) beansprouts

3 litres (6¼ pints) chicken stock

4 boneless, skin-on chicken
breasts, ideally corn-fed,
each about 200g (7oz)

6 tsp fish sauce

6 tsp sugar

3 tsp salt

3 chicken stock cubes, crumbled

3 tsp chicken fat or vegetable oil

1 tsp shrimp paste or umami paste

4 tbsp lemongrass chilli oil (see
page 180), or store-bought
chilli oil, plus extra to serve

FOR THE GARNISH

1 large red onion, thinly sliced
lengthways

10g (⅓oz) Thai basil

10g (⅓oz) Vietnamese mint (or
use regular mint), leaves picked

3 spring onions (scallions),
finely chopped

200g (7oz) banana blossom,
thinly sliced (optional)

200g (7oz) morning glory spinach
(water spinach), thinly sliced
(optional)

1 lime, quartered

Traditional dishes are special in many ways, and should be respected like a family heirloom passed down through the generations. I love knowing that I have sat at the same table, eating the same dish, as my grandad's grandad; it gives me a wonderful feeling of connection to my family and to my culture. Like a lot of families, we have a collective favourite dish, and for us it's Bún Bò Huế, a rich, spicy beef noodle broth from Huế, a city in the middle of Vietnam. It is a dish that will make me and my siblings immediately change plans and head home the moment we hear mum is preparing it.

The intricate layers of flavour in the broth are built up carefully through hours and hours of effort. Far too laborious to fit in to most people's busy lives and so it is generally reserved for special occasions. However, this noodle soup is far too good to only eat occasionally, so I set about creating an easy Bún Gà Huế. Using chicken instead of beef as the base, it becomes a lighter broth yet retains the depth and richness of flavour that it's renowned for and instead of 8–10 hours cooking time, this dish is ready in just over an hour!

I have been very careful in my development of this recipe, coming from a place with nothing but love and respect for the original. I hope my interpretation has done the dish's heritage justice and that it also inspires you to seek out and try the original inspiration.

Add the oil to a large frying pan over a high heat. Once hot, add the shallots, ginger and lemongrass, char until brown and set aside. Using the same pan, char the pineapple for at least 5 minutes until all sides are browned and set aside with the other charred ingredients.

Meanwhile, in a separate dry pan, toast the star anise and coriander seeds over a medium heat for 5 minutes, then put into a large tea/spice strainer (or tie up in a muslin/cheesecloth pouch) and set aside.

Cook the noodles according to the packet instructions, then drain and set aside.

RECIPE CONTINUES

Put the beansprouts into a heatproof bowl, add boiling water to cover and leave for a few seconds, then drain and set aside to dry.

Add the stock and 500ml (17fl oz/generous 2 cups) water to a large saucepan or stockpot, along with the charred ingredients and spice strainer or muslin with the star anise and coriander seeds, and bring to a boil. Add the chicken breasts and cook over a high heat for 5 minutes. Skim off any impurities that rise to the top of the broth and turn the heat down to simmer.

After 10 minutes, remove the chicken, place in a bowl of iced water for a couple of minutes, then tear or slice into strips. Set aside.

Continue to simmer the broth over a low heat for another 15 minutes, then remove the pineapple, ginger, lemongrass and spice strainer or muslin. Season with the fish sauce, sugar, salt, stock cubes, chicken fat (or vegetable oil) and shrimp paste (or umami paste), then pour in the chilli oil and continue to simmer until you're ready to serve. You want it piping hot!

Place the noodles in your serving bowls and add the red onions, beansprouts and shredded chicken, then pour over the broth.

Sprinkle with the garnish ingredients and serve with a wedge of lime, and maybe a little dish of extra chilli oil, if you like it spicy.

Chicken and Sweetcorn Egg Drop Soup

SERVES 4

COOKING TIME: 40 MINUTES

1 tbsp vegetable oil

10g (⅓oz) fresh ginger, half thinly sliced and half cut into thin matchsticks

4 spring onions (scallions): 2 left whole and 2 finely chopped

2 boneless, skinless chicken breasts, each about 300g (10½oz)

1.5 litres (3¼ pints) chicken stock

1 x 400g (14oz) can of creamed sweetcorn

1 x 200g (7oz) can of sweetcorn, drained

60g (2oz) cornflour (cornstarch)

120ml (4fl oz/½ cup) water

4 eggs, separated, yolks left intact and whites whipped until a little frothy

4 pinches of ground black pepper

1 red chilli, sliced

4 coriander (cilantro) stems, leaves and stems finely chopped

4 tsp crispy fried shallots (store-bought or see page 184)

FOR THE SEASONING

1 tsp salt

2 tsp fish sauce

2 tsp sugar

2 chicken stock cubes, crumbled

Hand-tearing the chicken breasts is a must for this recipe; it was always my job growing up and I took it very seriously as I knew that it was so worth the effort. The rough texture really helps to take this heart-warming, tasty chicken soup to a whole other level.

Add the oil to a medium pot and bring to a high heat. Add the sliced ginger and the whole spring onions (scallions) and char for 1 minute. Add the chicken breasts and continue to cook for a further 4 minutes, flipping the chicken halfway through.

Pour over the stock, cover with a lid and simmer for 15–20 minutes until the chicken is cooked through. Remove the chicken and check it's cooked – it should be 165°C (330°F) using a meat thermometer, or check there is no pink in the centre. Leave for 10 minutes to cool, then tear by hand into really thin strips.

Meanwhile, add both cans of sweetcorn and the seasoning ingredients to the broth and continue to simmer for 5 minutes.

Then add the torn chicken strips back in and stir. Mix the cornflour (cornstarch) and water together, add to the broth and simmer for 5 minutes.

Using a ladle, stir the soup and slowly pour in the whipped egg whites, noting that the faster you stir, the finer the egg ribbons; stir as fast as you are comfortable doing.

Serve the soup and add a raw egg yolk to the centre of each bowl. Lastly, sprinkle with the chopped spring onions, ginger matchsticks, black pepper, chilli, coriander (cilantro) and crispy fried shallots.

Prawn and Watercress Soup

SERVES 4

COOKING TIME: 40 MINUTES

250g (9oz) raw king prawns (shrimp), peeled and deveined

2 tbsp vegetable oil

3 garlic cloves, minced

400g (14oz) potatoes, peeled and diced

1 litre (2 pints) chicken stock

2 chicken stock cubes, crumbled

100g (3½oz) butter

200g (7oz) watercress

4 tsp coconut cream (or use double/heavy cream)

2 spring onions (scallions), finely chopped

4 tsp crispy fried shallots (store-bought or see page 184)

4 coriander (cilantro) stems, leaves and stems finely chopped

1 red chilli, sliced (optional)

FOR THE SEASONING

Pinch of salt

1 tsp ground black pepper

2 tsp fish sauce

1 tsp sugar

This is a traditional rural Vietnamese soup that only takes about 10 minutes to make. My take on this wonderful soup involves blitzing the ingredients to thicken it and adding coconut cream and a little butter to deepen and enrich the flavours. Perfect when served with a hot crusty baguette!

Put the prawns (shrimp) in a small bowl, add the seasoning ingredients and mix well. Roughly mince the prawns and set aside.

Add 1 tablespoon of the oil to a medium pot over a high heat and toss the garlic for a few seconds until brown. Add the potatoes and stock, then reduce to a simmer for 10–15 minutes until the potatoes are soft.

Add the crumbled stock cubes, butter and watercress and continue to simmer for 5 minutes, then take off the heat, pour into a food processor or blender and blitz until smooth.

Add the remaining oil to a small pan and toss the prawns over a high heat for 2–3 minutes until cooked through.

To serve, pour the soup into serving bowls and evenly scatter the prawns across the top. Add a teaspoon of cream to each bowl then sprinkle over the spring onions (scallions), crispy fried shallots and coriander (cilantro). Lastly, if you like spice, add a slice or two of red chilli and serve.

Coconut Crab Udon Soup

SERVES 4

COOKING TIME: 15 MINUTES

500ml (17fl oz/generous 2 cups) chicken stock

400ml (14fl oz) coconut milk

200ml (7fl oz) water

2 tbsp cream cheese (I use Philadelphia), optional

200g (7oz) mixture of brown and white crabmeat

½ tsp salt

2 chicken stock cubes, crumbled

20g (¾oz) cornflour (cornstarch)

2 x 200g (7oz) packets of ready-to-heat udon noodles

4 spring onions (scallions), finely chopped

4 coriander (cilantro) stems, leaves and stems finely chopped

4 Thai basil stems, leaves finely chopped

4 tsp crispy fried shallots (store-bought or see page 184)

4 pinches of ground black pepper

A rich and creamy soup with bouncy, chewy noodles and wonderful umami hits of crab, this is my quick and easy version of Bánh Canh Cua Nước Cốt Dừa. A dish so synonymous with my childhood that every time I eat it, I am instantly transported back to my village market with a bowl cupped in my hands. Always served by the same auntie, in the same spot, from the same simple cart. Always piping hot and always delicious!

Rather than a recipe, this feels more like I'm sharing the key to my happy place. Hopefully you will try it and join me there.

Put the chicken stock, coconut milk, water and the cream cheese (if using) into a saucepan and bring to the boil. Add the crabmeat, salt and crumbled stock cubes, then lower the heat to medium and cook for 2 minutes.

In a small bowl, mix the cornflour (cornstarch) and 40ml (scant 3 tbsp) water together, then pour into the soup and stir for 10 seconds.

Add the udon and cook for a further 3 minutes until the noodles are soft and bouncy, then add the spring onions (scallions) and remove from the heat.

Pour into your serving bowls and garnish with the herbs, crispy shallots and black pepper.

Lobster and Crab Tomato Noodle Soup

SERVES 4

COOKING TIME: 55 MINUTES

400g (14oz) vermicelli rice noodles

2 cooked lobsters, halved

6 spring onions (scallions), halved crossways

150g (5oz) fresh shiitake mushrooms

10g (⅓oz) coriander (cilantro), finely chopped

10g (⅓oz) Thai basil, leaves picked

10g (⅓oz) mint, leaves picked

1 lime, cut into 8 wedges

2 red chillies, thinly sliced

FOR THE RIÊU MIXTURE

100g (3½oz) shredded white crabmeat

1 x 160g (5½oz) can of minced crab in spices or mixed crabmeat

2 large eggs

250g (9oz) minced (ground) pork or chicken

1 tsp ground black pepper

2 tsp sugar

1 tsp salt

1 tsp fish sauce

This recipe is inspired by Bún Riêu Cua, a complex pork, crab and tomato broth with traditional toppings such as blood cakes and pigs' trotters. For this book I have removed hours of cooking time and swapped out those traditional toppings for lobster, so that it is the perfect dish for a special treat.

The recipe also calls for shrimp paste, which is widely available from East and Southeast Asian supermarkets or online. Umami paste is a good alternative.

My hope is that you enjoy this quick and easy adaptation of Bún Riêu Cua so much that one day you will try the traditional version. It is truly delicious.

Put all the riêu mixture ingredients into a small bowl, mix together and set aside. It should remain a little lumpy.

Cook the noodles according to the packet instructions, then drain and set aside.

Remove the lobster from its packaging and heat through according to the instructions.

Gather your broth ingredients together. Add the oil to a large saucepan or stockpot and bring to a high heat. Once hot, add the shallots and tomatoes and toss for 2–3 minutes until browned. Add the tomato purée and cook for another minute, then add the remaining broth ingredients and bring to the boil.

RECIPE CONTINUES

FOR THE BROTH

2 tbsp vegetable oil

5 red shallots, sliced lengthways

500g (1lb 2oz) cherry tomatoes on the vine

4 tbsp tomato purée (paste)

4 garlic cloves, minced

3 litres (6¼ pints) chicken stock

3 chicken stock cubes, crumbled

5 tsp sugar

4 tsp fish sauce

2 tsp salt

3 tsp chicken fat (or vegetable oil)

1 tsp shrimp paste or umami paste

While the broth is bubbling away, slowly and evenly pour in the riêu mixture so that it floats, roughly covering the surface as it cooks. Lower the heat and simmer for 20 minutes.

Add the spring onions (scallions) and mushrooms, cook for a further 5 minutes, then take off the heat.

Place the noodles in the bottom of the bowls and then add the coriander (cilantro), Thai basil and mint. Place the lobster halves on top and surround them with riêu mixture and the cherry tomatoes from the broth pot.

Pour over the delicious broth and serve with a couple of lime wedges, and a few slices of chilli, if you like.

Mushroom and Smoked Tofu Noodle Soup

4 tbsp vegetable oil

12 quail's eggs (or regular eggs)

200g (7oz) flat rice noodles

225g (8oz) firm smoked tofu (bean
curd), sliced into thin strips

200g (7oz) fresh woodland
mushrooms

1 large red onion, thinly sliced
lengthways

FOR THE BROTH

10 shallots (or two medium
onions), peeled and halved

100g (3½oz) fresh ginger, halved
and crushed

1 cinnamon stick

10 star anise

2 litres (4¼ pints) vegetable stock

3 vegetable stock cubes,
crumbled

6 tsp sugar

6 tsp soy sauce

3 tsp salt

Inspired by Phở aromatics, I wanted to create something light, yet flavoursome. Here, the aromas and flavours of the spices combined with the smokiness of tofu and the earthy flavours of the vegetables make for a delicious soul-warming soup.

Add 2 teaspoons of the oil to a large saucepan or stockpot over a high heat. Once hot, add the peeled shallots and ginger (with skin on), then char for 5 minutes until brown and set aside. Add the cinnamon stick and star anise and char for a further minute.

Pour the vegetable stock and 500ml (17fl oz/generous 2 cups) water into the pot and bring to the boil over a high heat. Skim off any impurities that rise to the top and turn the heat down to simmer for 25 minutes.

Meanwhile, bring a small saucepan of water to the boil and cook the quail's eggs for 3 minutes (or regular eggs for 6 minutes, for runny yolks). Remove and place straight into a bowl of iced water for a minute, then peel and set aside.

Cook the noodles according to the packet instructions, then drain and set aside.

Add the remaining oil to a small frying pan over a high heat. Once hot, add the tofu (bean curd) strips and toss for 2 minutes, add the mushrooms and toss for a further 30 seconds, then take off the heat and set aside.

RECIPE CONTINUES

FOR THE GARNISH

2 tbsp crispy fried shallots
 (store-bought or see page 184)

4 spring onions (scallions),
 finely chopped

20g (¾oz) Thai basil, leaves picked

10g (⅓oz) coriander (cilantro),
 finely chopped

1 lime, cut into 8 wedges

4 tbsp chilli oil, optional

Return to the broth pot and remove the spices, charred shallots and ginger. Skim any impurities off the top, then add the remaining broth ingredients. Leave to simmer while you start preparing your bowls.

Place the noodles in your serving bowls and put the mushrooms, tofu, eggs and sliced red onions on top. Pour over the piping hot broth and generously garnish with the crispy shallots, spring onions (scallions), Thai basil and coriander (cilantro).

Serve with a wedge or two of lime and a small bowl of chilli oil, for an extra kick.

Smoked Mackerel and Mushroom Rice Porridge

SERVES 4

COOKING TIME: 1 HOUR 20 MINUTES

4 large egg yolks

2 litres (4¼ pints) chicken stock (or use fish stock)

150g (5oz) jasmine rice, washed and drained

1 tsp salt, plus a pinch

1 tbsp vegetable oil

4 smoked mackerel fillets, each about 150g (5oz)

300g (10½oz) fresh woodland mushrooms

1 medium red onion, thinly sliced lengthways

2 pinches of sugar

3 tsp ground black pepper, plus a pinch

2 spring onions (scallions), finely chopped

4g (⅙oz) fresh ginger, finely cut into thin matchsticks

4 tsp crispy fried shallots (store-bought or see page 184)

4 tsp lemongrass chilli oil (see page 180), optional

FOR THE CURING MIXTURE

5 tbsp light soy sauce

4 tbsp water

2 tsp granulated sugar

The reality is that most days breakfast involves grabbing some toast and a coffee while my eyes are still half shut. However, my perfect breakfast, when I have time on my hands, is a comforting bowl of rice porridge (Cháo). It comes together easily and just requires a gentle simmer, so if you have a morning at home, this is the perfect recipe.

Here, I've tweaked the traditional Cháo by adding smoked mackerel, egg yolk and mushrooms, as it works so well with the porridge, and the flavour reminds me of my favourite Vietnamese dried fish, basa.

This is a great recipe if you have any leftover rice; it also cuts the rice cooking time down to just 10–15 minutes. Heat the rice with the stock until boiling, lower the heat and cook until your desired texture.

Put the curing mixture ingredients into a small bowl, mix together, then carefully place the egg yolks in the bowl. Cure in the fridge for 30 minutes, gently spooning the curing mixture over the yolks after 15 minutes.

Meanwhile, bring the stock to the boil in a large pan, add the rice and 1 teaspoon of the salt, then lower the heat and simmer for 1 hour.

Bring the vegetable oil to a medium heat in a small pan. Tear the mackerel into bite-sized pieces, then add to the pan along with the mushrooms and red onions. Sprinkle over the sugar, a pinch of salt and black pepper, then fry on a medium heat for 2 minutes until brown.

The broth will now be looking like porridge with a thick consistency and a mushy texture. Add more time if you prefer it thicker still.

To serve, pour a ladle of porridge into a large bowl, place the mackerel, mushrooms and onion and a cured egg yolk on top.

Garnish with the spring onions (scallions) and ginger. Sprinkle over the remaining black pepper and the crispy fried shallots, then drizzle over the lemongrass chilli oil, if you like.

SALADS & STIR-FRIES

Less is More

We've all had that realization at some point that the simplest things in life can bring us the most joy. For me it's that thrown-together salad that only takes a couple of minutes to make and is an absolute joy to eat. When fresh vegetables are prepared in a way that emphasizes their natural flavours and textures, and combined with a sauce that takes them to a new level, it's impossible not to love. As a chef, I am always seeking to showcase the natural flavours of ingredients, enhancing them where possible and making sure not to overpower the more subtle elements. Never is this more important than with salads and stir-fries, where the key is to embrace the essence of the vegetable and let nature's kick shine through!

Cooking, for me, has always been a celebration of ingredients. As a child I would watch grandma wait with anticipation to find out that day's offerings, and dinner was very much dependent on grandpa's luck fishing or mum's luck selling at the market.

Grandma would let me roam around the farm helping her gather the day's herbs and vegetables, allowing the odd cheeky nibble on a fruit here and there along the way. The whole village would operate on a zero-wastage policy, so it has been drummed into me from a very early age. Water spinach was a favourite, as I got to join grandma in the muddy water to pick it. She had a special hooked blade that she'd slash back and forth, which was mesmerizing to watch.

Depending on what the protein dish was for the day, grandma would often only have a few minutes to come up with something wonderful from her pantry. Creating in the moment was the norm. Of course, we would mostly have traditional meals, but her off-the-cuff dishes were unique every time and always delicious. Obviously no recipe was ever written down and probably not even given a second thought, as it wasn't 'a proper dish' or the process wasn't laborious enough to be worth sharing. How I wish I could go back in time with a pen and paper... although I'd probably just end up getting tamarind juice on it anyway.

This chapter introduces classic Southeast Asian ingredients that will be found in every Vietnamese larder. They are the Viet cook's go-to tools to liven up anything from a fresh salad to leftover noodles. There is no vegetable or fruit that needs ever to go to waste once you understand the process of balancing a homemade dressing. These recipes, while delicious themselves, should be used as inspiration for your own creations; they should encourage you to use whatever you have available. Have fun with the toppings, get creative and enjoy.

In my experience, there is a common misconception that a dish put together easily will not taste as good as one that takes hours. Well, this chapter aims to dispel that, and I hope that once you've cooked a couple of the recipes you will agree.

Blood Orange and Smoked Salmon Salad

SERVES 2

**PREPARATION TIME:
15 MINUTES**

3 blood oranges, peeled and cut
into 5mm (¼in) rounds

200g (7oz) smoked salmon, torn
into small pieces

100g (3½oz) French (breakfast)
radishes, thinly sliced

2 Persian cucumbers (or use 1
regular cucumber), thinly sliced

100ml (3½fl oz) nước chấm fish
sauce (see page 182)

5g (⅕oz) mint, leaves plucked

5g (⅕oz) coriander (cilantro),
finely chopped

1 tbsp crispy fried shallots
(store-bought or see page 184)

1 red chilli, thinly sliced

Blood orange season is far too short! My mission each year is to eat them in as many ways as possible from the start of the season to the end. From as far back as I can remember, I have always enjoyed cooking with fresh fruits and love the complexity of flavours that they bring to the plate.

This dish is particularly special to me as it was the very first time my mum actually asked to try something where the ingredients are raw! This dish is inspired by the Latin American dish Ceviche, but here I've added a hint of Vietnamese flavours.

Arrange the oranges evenly across a serving plate, along with the salmon pieces and sliced radishes and cucumber, then pour over the nước chấm fish sauce.

Top with the mint and coriander (cilantro), then sprinkle over the crispy fried shallots and chilli slices.

Crab Salad with Mango and Swede

SERVES 2

PREPARATION TIME:
15 MINUTES

1 small swede (rutabaga), peeled and cut into thin matchsticks

1 green (unripe) mango, peeled and cut into thin matchsticks

5g (⅕oz) Vietnamese mint (or use regular mint), leaves picked

5g (⅕oz) coriander (cilantro), roughly chopped

5g (⅕oz) Thai basil, leaves picked and roughly chopped

300ml (10fl oz/1¼ cups) tamarind fish sauce (see page 181)

100g (3½oz) shredded white crabmeat

1 tbsp lemongrass chilli oil (see page 180), optional

1 tsp crispy fried shallots (store-bought or see page 184)

10g (⅓oz) roasted unsalted peanuts, roughly crushed in a pestle and mortar

1 red chilli, thinly sliced

Green papayas are a staple in Vietnamese cuisine, as they are the perfect accompaniment to many of our dishes, including amazing crunchy salads such as this one. They are cheap to buy and easily accessible in Vietnam; at my grandma's house, papayas hang on a tree in the front yard all year round.

In the UK, supplies of green papaya are not constant and the price is high as a result, so when I have been stuck in the past I have replaced it, as I've done here, with the humble swede (rutabaga). I only realized after sharing the dish with my team at The Little Viet Kitchen that swede isn't considered a particularly exciting ingredient in the UK. Well, I beg to differ... step forward, mighty swede, this is your moment to shine!

Put the swede (rutabaga), mango, mint, coriander (cilantro) and Thai basil in a serving bowl. Pour over half the tamarind fish sauce and lightly toss together. Taste and then add more dressing to your liking. Don't worry about wastage here, as any leftover sauce can be kept for days in the fridge.

Remove any moisture from the crabmeat, if required, then liberally scatter across the salad.

Drizzle the crab with the lemongrass chilli oil, if using, then garnish with the crispy fried shallots, crushed peanuts and chilli slices.

Duck, Kohlrabi and Pink Grapefruit Salad

SERVES 2

COOKING TIME: 30 MINUTES

2 duck breasts, each about 250g (9oz)

2 pinches of salt

1 pink grapefruit, segmented

¼ cucumber, cut into thin matchsticks

1 green (unripe) mango, peeled and cut into thin matchsticks

1 kohlrabi, peeled and cut into thin matchsticks

FOR THE DRESSING

4 tbsp sweet chilli sauce

4 tbsp fish sauce

4 tbsp lime juice

4 tbsp water

20g (¾oz) fresh ginger, peeled and roughly chopped

1 bird's-eye chilli

10g (⅓oz) coriander (cilantro)

10g (⅓oz) Vietnamese mint (or use regular mint), leaves picked

Duck cooked medium-rare is not traditional in Vietnam, but I particularly enjoy how succulent a medium-rare duck breast can be. That said, feel free to cook it a little longer, if you prefer. Here I have paired it with pink grapefruit, as the acidity really cuts through the fattiness of the duck, and the bittersweet flavours complement it perfectly.

Preheat the oven to 180°C/350°F/Gas 4.

Place all the dressing ingredients in a food processor or blender and blitz for 20–25 seconds. Set aside.

Score the skin of the duck breasts in a diamond pattern and rub the salt onto the skin. Place skin-side down in an ovenproof frying pan, then bring to a low to medium heat and cook for 4–6 minutes, until the fat has rendered and the skin is golden and crispy. Transfer to the oven and cook for 5–6 minutes for medium-rare. Adjust the cooking times according to taste.

Remove from the oven and rest for 5 minutes before thinly slicing. Set aside.

Add the grapefruit, cucumber, mango and kohlrabi to a large bowl, pour over the dressing and mix together well.

Add the sliced duck to the bowl, and serve.

Lemongrass and Pineapple Beef Vermicelli Salad

SERVES 4

COOKING TIME: 30 MINUTES, PLUS MARINATING

500g (1lb 2oz) beef topside (top round)

200g (7oz) vermicelli rice noodles

1 cucumber, cut into thin matchsticks

3 carrots, ideally 1 yellow, 1 orange and 1 purple, cut into thin matchsticks

2 baby gem lettuce, finely shredded

80g (3oz) pea shoots

20g (¾oz) coriander (cilantro), roughly chopped

20g (¾oz) Thai basil, leaves roughly chopped

1 tsp vegetable oil

400ml (14fl oz) pineapple fish sauce (see page 181)

4 tsp crispy fried shallots (store-bought or see page 184)

40g (1½oz) roasted unsalted peanuts, roughly crushed in a pestle and mortar

FOR THE MARINADE

2 tbsp red chilli paste

2 tbsp garlic paste

2 tbsp lemongrass paste

2 tbsp fish sauce

2 tbsp oyster sauce

3 chicken stock cubes, crumbled

5 tbsp sesame oil

2 tbsp honey

1 tsp ground black pepper

If there's a dish that best shows off the intricacies of the flavours and textures of Vietnamese food, then this might be it. The contrasts are a delight: there's hot meat and cold sauce, soft noodles and crunchy peanuts, and, of course, a spicy sauce laced with sweet, sour, salty and bitter notes. It's a delight to the tastebuds!

Cut the beef lengthways into strips 5cm (2in) wide, then slice across the strips as thinly as you can.

Cook the noodles according to the packet instructions, then drain and set aside.

Put all the marinade ingredients into a large bowl and mix together well. Add the beef slices, then gently and evenly coat in the marinade, taking extra care as beef this thin is fragile. Place in the fridge for a minimum of 1 hour, but up to 3 hours for best results, taking it out to room temperature 30 minutes before cooking.

Before cooking the beef, place the noodles in the base of each serving bowl, then add the cucumber and carrot strips, along with the lettuce, pea shoots, coriander (cilantro) and Thai basil, then set aside.

Add the oil to a large frying pan over a high heat. When hot, add the beef (in 2 batches for best results) and cook for 4–6 minutes until well done. (The beef may be a little burnt around the edges from the honey and that's perfect.)

Serve the beef on top of the vegetables, then pour over the pineapple fish sauce and sprinkle over the crispy fried shallots and peanuts to finish.

Morning Glory Beef Salad

SERVES 4

COOKING TIME: 30 MINUTES, PLUS MARINATING

200g (7oz) morning glory spinach (water spinach), or other soft green leaves such as rocket (arugula), watercress, kale, wild garlic

500g (1lb 2oz) beef topside (top round)

5g (⅕oz) Thai basil, leaves roughly chopped

5g (⅕oz) coriander (cilantro), roughly chopped

5g (⅕oz) mint, leaves picked

1 large red onion, thinly sliced lengthways

200ml (7fl oz) nước chấm fish sauce (see page 182)

1 tbsp vegetable oil

1 tbsp crispy fried shallots (store-bought or see page 184)

50g (1¾oz) roasted salted peanuts, roughly crushed

1 red chilli, thinly sliced

FOR THE MARINADE

2 red chillies, minced

4 garlic cloves, minced

4 lemongrass stalks, minced

2 tbsp fish sauce

1 tbsp light soy sauce

1 tbsp oyster sauce

1 tbsp sugar

4 tbsp sesame oil

This simple divine salads works well with morning glory or other soft green leaves, everything from watercress to kale. It's not only versatile, but extremely delicious.

Wash the morning glory (water spinach) or other soft green leaves and slice into thin strips, then soak in cold (tap) water for 15 minutes to curl. Drain and set aside.

Cut the beef lengthways into strips 5cm (2in) wide, then slice across the strips as thinly as you can.

Put the sliced beef into a bowl, add all the marinade ingredients and rub evenly into the slices. Place in the fridge for 1 hour, taking it out to room temperature 30 minutes before cooking.

Put the morning glory, Thai basil, coriander (cilantro), mint, red onion and nước chấm fish sauce into a bowl, toss gently together and set aside.

Add the vegetable oil to a small frying pan over a high heat. When hot, add the beef and all the marinade and cook for 3–5 minutes until browned.

Serve the beef on top of the salad and sprinkle over the crispy fried shallots, peanuts and chilli slices.

Pan-Tossed Asparagus with Lemongrass and Mushroom

SERVES 2

COOKING TIME: 10 MINUTES

250g (9oz) asparagus stems, trimmed

1 tsp vegetable oil

1 lemongrass stalk, minced

1 red onion, finely diced

1 king oyster mushroom, finely diced

1 medium carrot, finely diced

½ tsp salt

1 tsp sugar

2 garlic cloves, minced

3 tsp butter

1 red bird's-eye chilli, minced

When asparagus is in season, I find myself eating almost nothing else. This recipe aims to keep as much of the wonderful natural flavour and goodness of asparagus in the dish as possible, with just a little kick of lemongrass and chilli to spice it up!

Add the asparagus stems to a bowl, pour over boiling water and soak for 20 seconds. Drain, then immediately place in a bowl of iced water for 20 seconds. Drain and set aside.

Add the oil to a frying pan and bring to a low heat. Add the lemongrass, onion, mushroom, carrot, salt and sugar and cook for 30 seconds, then add the garlic, butter and chilli and cook for a further 30 seconds until the butter has melted.

Add the asparagus stems to the pan, toss for 30 seconds until they are fully coated in the melted butter, then serve.

Pork and Purple Broccoli Udon

SERVES 2

COOKING TIME: 20 MINUTES

2 x 200g (7oz) packets of ready-to-heat udon noodles

200g (7oz) purple sprouting broccoli, cut into 5cm (2in) pieces

1 tbsp vegetable oil

500g (1lb 2oz) minced (ground) pork

1 large red onion, cut into 2cm (¾in) wedges

2 tsp lemongrass chilli oil (see page 180), optional

2 tsp crispy fried shallots (store-bought or see page 184)

2 spring onions (scallions), finely chopped

3 coriander (cilantro) stems, leaves and stems finely chopped

FOR THE SAUCE

4 tsp oyster sauce

2 tsp light soy sauce

2 tsp sugar

1 tsp ground black pepper

1 tsp white wine vinegar

1 tsp lemongrass paste

1 tsp garlic paste

1 tsp chilli paste

2 tsp sesame oil

I have a special love for rice and noodles, all the types you can think of, and one of my favourites is bánh canh noodles. These are quite difficult to source in the UK, but fortunately udon, which is readily available, has a very similar taste and chewy texture; like bánh canh, it is delicious and super-easy to cook with. This versatile recipe is very quick to put together, and takes full advantage of that amazing udon texture by making sure the sauce clings on to every strand!

Put the noodles in a heatproof bowl, pour boiling water over them to cover and soak for 5 minutes, then drain and set aside. Repeat the process with the broccoli pieces, soaking for 2 minutes before draining.

Mix all the sauce ingredients together in a bowl and set aside.

Add the oil to a large frying pan and bring to a high heat. Add the pork and pour over the sauce. Mix well and fry for 5–7 minutes, stirring to break up any clumps, until light brown. Tip into a bowl and set aside.

Over a high heat, add the broccoli and onion to the same pan and char for 1 minute. Add the drained noodles and continue to cook for a further minute.

Add the pork and sauce back into the pan and toss everything together for another minute.

Serve, then drizzle over the lemongrass chilli oil, if using, and sprinkle over the crispy fried shallots and spring onions (scallions). Lastly, dress with the coriander (cilantro) and enjoy.

Pineapple Smashed Cucumber Salad

SERVES 4

PREPARATION TIME: 5 MINUTES

8–10 Persian cucumbers
(or 4–5 regular cucumbers)

4 tbsp pineapple fish sauce (see
page 181, or make it vegan with
the chilli and garlic soy sauce on
page 184)

2 tbsp crispy fried shallots
(store-bought or see page 184)

10g (⅓oz) Vietnamese mint (or
use regular mint), leaves picked

20g (¾oz) Thai basil, finely
chopped

**Perfect as a refreshing side salad, a quick snack or as part of
a family-style meal, this dish is really easy to make and can
be prepared in bulk and stored in your pantry for weeks!**

Halve the cucumbers lengthways, then lightly smash using a
rolling pin.

Cut into thick slices, place in a bowl and pour the pineapple fish
sauce over.

Ideally wait for an hour for the flavours to infuse, then scatter over
the crispy shallots and fresh herbs.

Thinly Sliced Beef Fillet Salad

SERVES 4

COOKING TIME: 20 MINUTES

400g (14oz) beef fillet
(ideally organic)

4 tbsp pineapple fish sauce
(see page 181)

2 limes, halved

FOR THE GARNISH

20g (¾oz) coriander (cilantro),
finely chopped

20g (¾oz) Vietnamese mint (or
use regular mint), finely chopped

20g (¾oz) Thai basil, finely
chopped

2 red chillies, sliced

4 tsp crispy fried shallots
(store-bought or see page 184)

40g (1½oz) roasted unsalted
peanuts, roughly crushed in
a pestle and mortar

This is my take on the classic Vietnamese Bò Tái Chanh, a dish similar to Italian Carpaccio. It has often been my choice for the opening course of my supper clubs, as it's such a standout dish. Carpaccio lends itself well to infusions of different flavours and, as such, is a wonderful vessel to showcase the layering and seasoning that Vietnamese cuisine has to offer.

Cut the beef lengthways into strips 5cm (2in) wide, then slice across the strips as thinly as you possibly can. It is important that the meat is sliced very thinly so that the sauce cures the meat, otherwise it will be chewy. If you have time, a tip here is to wrap the strips in clingfilm (plastic wrap) and put in the freezer for 30 minutes. This makes precision slicing so much easier!

Place the sliced beef down flat in a single layer on 4 plates that have a rim, spreading fully across the plate. Pour the pineapple fish sauce over the beef, tilting the plate around to ensure that every piece is completely coated. Leave to cure for 5 minutes, then squeeze half a lime across each plate and leave to cure for a further 5 minutes.

Garnish with the coriander (cilantro), mint, Thai basil and chilli slices, then sprinkle over the crispy fried shallots and peanuts, and you are ready. Enjoy the compliments!

Spicy Steak with a Pear, Rocket and Watercress Salad

SERVES 4

COOKING TIME: 20 MINUTES, PLUS MARINATING

2 rib-eye steaks, each about 300g (10½oz)

½ tsp vegetable oil

100g (3½oz) watercress leaves

90g (3oz) rocket (arugula) leaves

1 red onion, thinly sliced lengthways

2 blush pears (as firm as possible), thinly sliced

FOR THE MARINADE

2 tsp light soy sauce

1 tsp fish sauce

4 tsp sesame oil

1 tsp chilli paste

2 tsp garlic paste

4 tsp oyster sauce

2 tsp ground black pepper

60ml (4 tbsp/¼ cup) sweet chilli sauce

20ml (1 tbsp plus 1 tsp) lime juice

FOR THE DRESSING

60ml (4 tbsp/¼ cup) olive oil

1 tsp red chilli paste

1 tsp garlic paste

1 tsp caster (superfine) sugar

60ml (4 tbsp/¼ cup) balsamic vinegar

20ml (1 tbsp plus 1 tsp) light soy sauce

3 coriander (cilantro) stems, leaves and stems finely chopped

This recipe is inspired by the tasty Vietnamese classic Bò Lúc Lắc, or 'shaking beef'. The beef and marinade are traditional, and here, I have paired the watercress salad with bitter and peppery rocket (arugula) and delightfully sweet blush pears, and dressed it all with a tangy balsamic sauce.

Put the steaks into a bowl along with all the marinade ingredients and massage well, ensuring they are fully covered. Cover and leave in the fridge for a minimum of 1 hour or, for best results, 3 hours, taking them out to room temperature 30 minutes before cooking. Wipe off as much of the marinade (reserve the marinade) as possible and set aside.

Add the oil to a medium frying pan over a high heat. When hot, add the marinated steaks and toss for 1 minute until medium-rare. Take off the heat and leave to rest.

Put all the dressing ingredients into a small bowl, mix together well and set aside.

Once rested, slice the steaks into strips.

Gently toss the watercress and rocket (arugula) together, then place on a large serving plate. Add the onion and pears on top, then pour over the dressing, according to taste.

Add the reserved marinade to a pan over a medium heat for 1 minute to warm through. Place the steak on top of the salad and drizzle over the marinade to finish.

Bánh Xèo, Sizzling Seafood Pancakes

MAKES 8 LARGE PANCAKES

COOKING TIME: 7 MINUTES PER PANCAKE, PLUS PREPPING AND CHILLING

300g (10½oz) hot-smoked salmon, flaked

20 crab sticks (400g/14oz in total), shredded into thin strips

40 cooked shelled king prawns (shrimp)

8 tsp vegetable oil

1 kohlrabi, peeled and cut into thin matchsticks

2 carrots, cut into thin matchsticks

FOR THE BATTER

200g (7oz) rice flour

100g (3½oz) cornflour (cornstarch)

400ml (14fl oz) coconut milk

550ml (19fl oz/2¼ cups) sparkling water

1 tsp salt

3 tsp sugar

3 tsp ground turmeric

20g (¾oz) chives, finely chopped

TO SERVE

2 baby gem lettuce, leaves separated

1 red chicory (endive), leaves separated

200g (7oz) carrot and daikon pickle (see page 180)

20g (¾oz) mint, leaves picked

20g (¾oz) coriander (cilantro)

20g (¾oz) Thai basil, leaves picked

400ml (14fl oz) nước chấm fish sauce (see page 182)

This crispy stuffed pancake ticks all the boxes for a winning dish; delicious, colourful and fragrant, it also sounds so appetizing that the dish is named after the noise it makes while cooking!

The real beauty of this dish is how versatile it can be without compromising its integrity. It is often served with pork and prawns (shrimp), and here I've used more seafood. Make it vegan, pescatarian or meaty by mixing up the filling to suit your taste.

Put all the batter ingredients except the chives into a large bowl and mix until smooth. Then add the chopped chives and place in the fridge for an hour to set.

Heat a 24cm (9½in) non-stick frying pan over a high heat and add the salmon, crab and prawns (shrimp) to the dry pan, fry for 15 seconds, then set aside.

Using the same pan, heat 1 teaspoon of oil over a high heat. Pour in a ladle of the batter mixture, just enough to cover the whole pan with a thin layer. Add a small handful of the kohlrabi and carrots to the middle and then scatter the salmon, crab and prawns across the whole pancake. Immediately lower the heat and put the lid on for 2½ minutes, to cook the centre and slowly crisp the outside.

Remove the lid and continue to cook over a low heat for a further 3½ minutes until the pancake has that signature golden yellow colour.

Fold the pancake in half, remove from the pan and serve immediately, repeating to use up the remaining ingredients and make the rest of the pancakes.

This is traditionally served with the lettuce, any herbs, salad and pickles laid out on the table to share, with a small bowl of nước chấm per person. You can use a lettuce leaf to wrap up the serving ingredients along with some pancake, before dipping into the fish sauce.

MAIN DISHES

Rice is Life

If asked for the one thing I couldn't live without, it most definitely is rice, both figuratively and literally. After all, I am the granddaughter of rice farmers from the Mekong Delta, the region known as 'the rice bowl' and one of the world's largest producers and exporters of this precious grain.

It would seem that I was destined to love rice, and since my dad has never gone a day in his life without eating it, and that it's also the favourite food of my two-year-old son – whose Vietnamese name Xôi literally translates as 'sticky rice' – it's safe to assume that it's probably in my blood.

Growing up in Vietnam, as a happy child running around the farm, it always felt as though food was everywhere, but the reality was quite different. The best rice and vegetables would always go to the market to be sold, while our dinner often consisted of broken rice and anything mum hadn't managed to sell that day.

I have always believed that the most creative cooks are those with the least to work with; it forces you to make the most of ingredients and techniques. Take rice: from this humble grain, we get many types of noodles, rice paper, rice rolls, rice cakes, dumplings, pancakes and all those gorgeous savoury-sweet desserts, and this is just in Vietnam! If you travel around the rest of Asia, you will find countless other ingenious uses for it.

Rice is a wonderful absorber of sauces and the perfect carrier of flavours. Add rice to almost any starter and, voilà, you have a main! But my favourite thing about it is that it has the most wonderful ability to balance a dish. From the lightest vegetable stir-fries to the most intense curries and richest of stews, you add a portion of rice and it will even out the flavours perfectly.

Most of the dishes in this chapter can be served with a portion of fluffy rice as a delicious dinner, or as they are as a small plate, it's completely up to you.

Baked Tamarind Tiger Prawns

SERVES 4

COOKING TIME: 35 MINUTES

12 raw tiger prawns (shrimp),
shells and heads on, rinsed
and drained

2 tsp butter

1 tbsp vegetable oil

1 tbsp sesame oil

1 whole garlic bulb

6 coriander (cilantro) stems,
leaves and stems finely chopped

3 dill stems, finely chopped

1 red chilli, thinly sliced

1 lime, cut into wedges, to serve

FOR THE SAUCE

3 tbsp vegetable oil

6 tbsp sweet chilli sauce

2 tbsp tamarind paste

4 tbsp fish sauce

6 tbsp water

A showstopper dish! When you've not got much time to create something fancy, this should be your go-to. It's a very forgiving recipe with minimal prep, and it's almost impossible to get wrong. Just make sure you get the freshest prawns you can find and the rest will take care of itself.

Preheat the oven to 200°C/400°F/Gas 6.

Put the prawns (shrimp) on a baking tray and evenly rub the butter, vegetable oil and sesame oil onto them. Add the garlic bulb to a separate tray and bake the prawns for 15–20 minutes, until pink, and the garlic for 30 minutes, until soft.

Meanwhile, put all the sauce ingredients into a small saucepan and place over a medium heat for 2 minutes. When you see bubbles starting to form, turn off the heat and set aside.

Arrange the prawns on a plate, pour over the sauce and squeeze those amazing roasted garlic cloves out of their skins, on top of the prawns. Sprinkle over the coriander (cilantro), dill and chilli slices and serve with a lime wedge, and jasmine rice if you'd like to turn it into a main course.

Oyster and Peppercorn Rib-eye Steak and Egg

SERVES 1

COOKING TIME: 15 MINUTES, PLUS MARINATING

1 rib-eye steak, 250–300g (9–10½oz), cut into 3cm (1¼in) cubes

½ medium red onion, thinly sliced

2 tsp sugar

1 lime, halved

6 cherry tomatoes

1 tbsp vegetable oil

2 medium eggs

20g (¾oz) watercress

¼ cucumber, cut into thin matchsticks

1 spring onion (scallion), thinly sliced

FOR THE MARINADE

2 tsp oyster sauce

2 tsp light soy sauce

3 garlic cloves, minced

1 tsp sugar

5 tsp sesame oil

1 tsp rice wine vinegar

1 tsp black peppercorns

FOR THE DIP (ADJUST QUANTITIES ACCORDING TO TASTE)

20ml (1½ tbsp) light soy sauce

1 red chilli, finely chopped

5g (⅕oz) each of salt and crushed black peppercorns

This is one of those dishes that magically draws all the people in the house to the kitchen when you start cooking. The quantities given here are for one, so multiply up if you are serving more.

Place the steak in a mixing bowl, add all the marinade ingredients and mix well. Leave in the fridge for a minimum of 1 hour, and up to 3 hours for full flavour. Bring to room temperature before cooking.

To make the onion pickle, add the red onion and sugar to a small bowl, then squeeze over one lime half, mix well and set aside in the fridge.

Mix together the dip ingredients and set aside.

Heat a medium frying pan over a high heat. Add the tomatoes and char for 3 minutes, turning halfway, until the skins break. Remove and set aside. Add the oil to the pan and fry the eggs until done to your liking, then remove and set aside. Make sure the pan is hot, then add the beef cubes and shake and toss! For medium-rare, shake and toss for 30–40 seconds.

Put the watercress and cucumber on your serving plate, then place the piping hot beef cubes on top, adding the charred tomato and onion pickle beside it. Lastly, place the fried eggs on the meat, sprinkle the spring onion (scallion) over the whole dish and add the remaining lime half for garnish.

Serve as it is as a small plate, or with a bowl of fluffy jasmine rice as a main, with the dip alongside.

Beef and Oxtail Stew

SERVES 6–8

COOKING TIME: 3½ HOURS, PLUS MARINATING

1kg (2lb 3oz) stewing beef, cubed

500g (1lb 2oz) oxtail, chopped

2 tbsp vegetable oil

500ml (17fl oz/generous 2 cups) beef stock

750ml (25⅓fl oz) coconut water

100g (3½oz) vermicelli rice noodles

100g (3½oz) beansprouts

60g (2oz) cornflour (cornstarch)

120ml (4fl oz/½ cup) water

300g (10½oz) baby carrots, trimmed

200g (7oz) French radishes, trimmed

200g (7oz) fresh shiitake mushrooms

25g (1oz) Thai basil stems, chopped

25g (1oz) coriander (cilantro) stems, leaves and stems chopped

4 tsp crispy fried shallots (store-bought or see page 184)

In Vietnam, this is a dish usually reserved for family gatherings and celebrations, due its rich and decadent flavours. Inspired by the traditional Bò Kho, which is typically more of a broth than a stew, this wonderfully comforting recipe is savoury and salty with a subtle contrasting sweetness from the coconut. My tip would be to make enough to last the whole week, as it only gets better when reheated.

Mix all the marinade ingredients together in a large bowl. Add the stewing beef and oxtail and rub the marinade in thoroughly before covering and placing in the fridge for 3 hours, or overnight if possible.

Preheat the oven to 150°C/300°F/Gas 2.

Add the oil to a large frying pan over a high heat. When hot, add the meat with the marinade and toss for 8–10 minutes until all sides are seared and golden brown around the edges. Transfer the meat to an ovenproof dish, add the stock and coconut water, cover with a lid and cook in the oven for 2½ hours.

Meanwhile, cook the noodles according to the packet instructions, then drain and set aside.

Put the beansprouts into a bowl, add boiling water to cover and leave for a few seconds, then drain and set aside to dry.

FOR THE MARINADE

2 tbsp lemongrass paste

2 tbsp ginger paste

2 tbsp garlic paste

1 tbsp tomato paste

3 tbsp fish sauce

1 tbsp five-spice powder

3 tbsp brown sugar

1 tbsp ground black pepper

1 tbsp chilli powder

1 tbsp ground annatto seeds
   (or paprika)

TO SERVE

1 lime, cut into 8 wedges

Crusty baguette

In a small bowl, mix the cornflour (cornstarch) and water together and set aside.

Remove the dish from the oven, add the carrots and radishes and stir in the cornflour mixture. Put back in the oven to cook for a further 25 minutes, before adding the mushrooms and cooking for a further 5 minutes.

Place the noodles in your serving bowls and pour over the stew. Dress with the beansprouts, Thai basil and coriander (cilantro), then sprinkle over the crispy fried shallots and serve with a wedge of lime.

Lastly, a Vietnamese stew is never complete without a crispy baguette, so plate up and start dipping!

Bò Kho-style Steak and Lemongrass Pie

SERVES 6

COOKING TIME: 3 HOURS, PLUS MARINATING

1kg (2lb 3oz) stewing beef, cubed

2 tbsp vegetable oil

500ml (17fl oz/generous 2 cups) beef stock

330ml (11fl oz) coconut water

2 tsp tomato paste

1 tsp chilli powder

2 tsp ground annatto seeds (or paprika)

200g (7oz) baby carrots, trimmed

200g (7oz) shallots, peeled

1 x 320g (11¼oz) sheet of puff pastry

1 egg yolk

FOR THE MARINADE

4 tsp lemongrass paste

2 tsp ginger paste

2 tsp garlic paste

4 tsp fish sauce

2 tsp five-spice powder

4 tsp brown sugar

2 tsp ground black pepper

4 tbsp sesame oil

I recently went through a stage of making everything into a pie, as I discovered pre-made pastry at my local supermarket. This particular recipe is like a Vietnamese Bò Kho – a traditional, rich and comforting beef stew – meets a classic steak pie, and it's a match made in heaven! I hope you enjoy it as much as I do.

Place all the marinade ingredients in a large bowl and mix together well. Add the beef and evenly rub in the marinade. Cover and leave in the fridge for a minimum of 30 minutes, or overnight for best results.

Preheat the oven to 150°C/300°F/Gas 2.

Add the vegetable oil to a medium frying pan over a high heat. When hot, add the steak, along with any marinade, and sear for 5–8 minutes until golden brown all over.

Put the stock and coconut water into a baking dish that has a lid, along with the tomato paste, chilli powder and ground annatto seeds, then stir together well.

Add the seared beef, carrots and shallots, cover with the lid and bake for 2 hours. Take out of the oven, transfer to a pie dish and cool to room temperature.

Increase the oven temperature to 200°C/400°F/Gas 6.

Once the filling has cooled, lay the pastry over the dish, not forgetting to add your personal artistic touch to the top; a hole or slit for the steam will work nicely. Brush over the egg yolk and bake for 25–30 minutes until the centre is piping hot and the crust is golden. Serve with jasmine rice.

Baked Sea Bass with Mango and Clementine

SERVES 2

COOKING TIME: 25 MINUTES

1 tbsp melted butter

1 whole sea bass (or use fillets), about 270g (9½oz), gutted and descaled

1 tbsp salt

5g (⅒oz) Vietnamese mint leaves (or use regular mint), finely chopped

5 coriander (cilantro) stems, leaves and stems finely chopped

5 Thai basil stems, leaves finely chopped

2 spring onions (scallions), finely chopped

1 tbsp crispy fried shallots (store-bought or see page 184)

150g (5oz) roasted unsalted peanuts, roughly crushed in a pestle and mortar

1 red chilli, sliced

1 lime, cut into wedges, to serve

FOR THE SAUCE

1 unripe mango, peeled and diced

6 tbsp sweet chilli sauce

6 tbsp fish sauce

175ml (6fl oz/¾ cup) water

3 tbsp lime juice or white wine vinegar

Juice of 8 clementines, plus a few segments to serve

This recipe is perfect for a family dinner when served with rice and is always guaranteed to impress while actually requiring very little effort.

Preheat the oven to 200°C/400°F/Gas 6.

Brush a baking tray with the butter. Put the whole fish on the tray and rub all over with the salt. Bake for 20–25 minutes, depending on the size of your fish, then increase the heat to 230°C/400°F/Gas 8 and bake for an extra minute or two. You are aiming for really crispy skin, so keep your eye on it. Remove and keep warm. If using fillets, bake for 8–10 minutes at 200°C/400°F/Gas 6.

Put the diced mango in a dry saucepan and bring to a medium heat. Cook for 1 minute, then add the remaining sauce ingredients and cook for a further 2 minutes. When bubbles start to form, take off the heat and set aside.

Serve the fish and pour over the mango and clementine sauce. Sprinkle on the mint, coriander (cilantro), Thai basil, spring onions (scallions) and crispy shallots. Finish with the crushed peanuts and chilli slices, and serve with a lime wedge.

Ginger Poussin and Turmeric Rice

SERVES 2

COOKING TIME: 45 MINUTES, PLUS SOAKING

2 poussins, cleaned (see intro)

2 thick slices of lemon

2 garlic cloves, crushed

Thumb-sized piece of fresh ginger, crushed

2 lemongrass stalks, crushed

2 spring onions (scallions), bulb ends crushed

200ml (7fl oz) ginger fish sauce (see page 182)

40g (1½oz) carrot and daikon pickle (see page 180)

4 coriander (cilantro) stems, leaves and stems chopped

4 Vietnamese mint, stems (or use regular mint), leaves picked

2 tsp crispy fried shallots (store-bought or see page 184)

FOR THE TURMERIC RICE

200g (7oz) jasmine rice

1 tbsp vegetable oil

3 garlic cloves, minced

5g (⅛oz) fresh ginger, minced

4 shallots, thinly sliced lengthways

1 tsp ground turmeric

1 chicken stock cube, crumbled

2 tsp butter

1 tsp fish sauce

320ml (11fl oz) chicken stock

FOR THE MARINADE

2 tsp ground turmeric

2 tbsp sesame oil

2 tsp honey

2 tsp fish sauce

2 tsp oyster sauce

2 chicken stock cubes, crumbled

This is a dish perfect for two people. Inspired by the classic Hội An Chicken Rice, an incredibly delicious dish, this recipe makes use of juicy and succulent poussin and, here, the meat is baked for extra moisture.

Soak the rice in cold water for 30 minutes, then rinse, drain and set aside.

Preheat the oven to 220°C/430°F/Gas 7.

Put all the marinade ingredients into a bowl and mix together well. Massage evenly into the poussins, making sure not to miss any folds or crevices.

Stuff each bird with a lemon slice and the garlic, ginger, lemongrass and spring onions (scallions), then tie the legs together with a piece of string and place on a baking tray. Cook for 30–35 minutes, until cooked through and a thermometer reads 75°C (167°F) at the centre of the breast. Take out of the oven and rest for 10 minutes.

Meanwhile, for the turmeric rice, add the oil to a pan over a medium heat. Once hot, add the garlic, ginger and shallots. Toss for 30 seconds, then add the rice, turmeric, crumbled stock cube, butter and fish sauce. Mix well until the rice is fully yellow and fry, stirring, for 15 minutes. If you have a rice cooker, tip this in with the chicken stock and cook until the liquid is absorbed and the rice fluffy. Alternatively, bring it to boil in the stock, over a medium heat, then lower to a simmer and close the lid for approximately 8–10 minutes until the rice is soft, dry and fluffy. Remove from the heat and keep the lid on for a further 15 minutes before serving.

Tear the meat off the poussins and serve, or prepare the traditional way: leave the bones in and simply chop into pieces.

Serve the turmeric rice, add the poussin on top and pour over a generous amount of the ginger fish sauce. Add some carrot and daikon pickle and garnish with the coriander (cilantro), mint and a sprinkling of crispy fried shallots.

Rack of Lamb with a Papaya and Red Onion Salsa

SERVES 4

COOKING TIME: 40 MINUTES, PLUS MARINATING

1 rack of lamb, about 450g (1lb)

1 tbsp vegetable oil

FOR THE SALSA

2 ripe (yellow) papayas, diced (see intro)

1 large red onion, diced

3 Vietnamese mint stems (or use regular mint), leaves finely chopped

3 coriander (cilantro) stems, leaves and stems finely chopped

3 Thai basil stems, leaves finely chopped

4 tbsp pineapple fish sauce (see page 181)

FOR THE MARINADE

2 tsp fish sauce

1 tsp lemongrass paste

1 tsp ginger paste

1 tsp garlic paste

1 tsp chilli paste

1 tsp light soy sauce

1 tsp dark soy sauce

3 tsp sesame oil

1 tsp sugar

100g (3½oz) softened butter

Cooking a rack of lamb at home might seem daunting, but in this recipe, it couldn't be simpler. Simply marinate the meat and then pop it in the oven!

A rack of lamb is so delicious on its own that I never want to add too much to it; the flavour of the meat stands up with minimal seasoning. However, a simple ripe papaya salsa adds another layer of taste that really helps to elevate it to another level. This is definitely one to pull out at a dinner party with friends!

If you can't get hold of papaya, any fruit that is sweet, but not too soft, will work just as well. Honeydew melon, nectarine, mango or even watermelon would all work nicely.

Place all the marinade ingredients in a small bowl and mix together well. Evenly rub the marinade into the rack of lamb. Leave for 1 hour or, for perfect results, overnight in the fridge, taking it out to room temperature an hour before cooking.

Preheat the oven to 200°C/400°F/Gas 6.

Put the vegetable oil in a baking tray. Place the lamb rack in the tray and cook for 10 minutes, then reduce the oven temperature to 180°C/350°F/Gas 4 and cook for a further 10 minutes. For best results, check the temperature of the meat with a thermometer: 52°C (125°F) for rare and 57°C (135°F) for medium. Remove the lamb from the oven and rest for 5–10 minutes, to ensure the meat is beautifully juicy.

Meanwhile, make the salsa. Add the papaya, onion, mint, coriander (cilantro) and Thai basil to a bowl. Pour in the pineapple fish sauce and mix together gently, as ripe papaya is delicate.

Cut the lamb rack into individual portions and pour over the papaya salsa to serve, alongside some jasmine rice, if you like.

Salt and Pepper Five-Spice Duck in a Clementine and Onion Soy Sauce

SERVES 2

COOKING TIME: 25 MINUTES

2 duck breasts, each about
   250g (9oz)

1 tsp salt

1 tsp crushed black peppercorns

1 tsp five-spice powder

2 tsp crispy fried shallots
   (store-bought or see page 184),
   to garnish

FOR THE SAUCE

3–4 baby onions, peeled
   and halved

Zest and juice of 2 large
   clementines

3 tbsp sugar

2 tbsp light soy sauce

1 tbsp sesame oil

1 tsp crushed black peppercorns

1 tsp rice wine vinegar

This is one of those recipes where it's all about enhancing the hero ingredient, and the focus here is the succulent beautiful duck breast. The sweetness and subtle sourness of the clementine, combined with the warmth and umami of the five-spice marinade, perfectly heighten the flavours of the duck. Partnered with your favourite carb or greens, the duck will remain the star of the show!

Preheat the oven to 180°C/350°F/Gas 4.

Score the skin of the duck breasts in a diamond pattern and rub the salt, pepper and five-spice powder evenly across the skin. Place skin-side down in an ovenproof frying pan and set over a low to medium heat. Cook for 4–6 minutes, until the fat has rendered and the skin is golden and crispy.

Transfer the pan to the oven and cook for 5–6 minutes for medium, adjusting the cooking time according to taste. Remove from the oven and rest for 5 minutes before serving.

Meanwhile, place the baby onion halves cut-side down in a small saucepan and char over a high heat for 1 minute. Add the remaining sauce ingredients and cook for 4–6 minutes, stirring occasionally, until the sauce thickens to the consistency of double (heavy) cream.

Cut the duck breast into thick slices and pour over the sauce. Serve along with those deliciously soaked onions and a sprinkle of crispy fried shallots.

Salted Lemongrass Hake

SERVES 2

COOKING TIME: 15 MINUTES, PLUS MARINATING

2 hake fillets, each 300g (10½oz), rinsed in cold water and patted dry

1 tbsp vegetable oil

2 tsp cornflour (cornstarch)

4 Thai basil sprigs, leaves picked

1 spring onion (scallion), finely sliced into strips

lemongrass chilli oil (see page 180), or store-bought chilli oil, to serve (optional)

FOR THE MARINADE

4 lemongrass stalks, minced

1 red chilli, minced

3 garlic cloves, minced

2 tbsp sesame oil

2 tsp salt

1 tsp fish sauce

1 chicken stock cube, crumbled

This is pure nostalgia for me; growing up, my grandma would make this all the time and it was a firm favourite. This style of cooking fish is popular for a few reasons: the infusion of salt means it keeps for longer and, of course, it's delicious. This recipe only uses a quarter of the traditional quantity of salt (so you know what to do if you're a salt lover!).

I've chosen hake here because the meaty texture works perfectly and the natural flavours of the fish really shine through. Cod, bass or sea bream also work very well, and if you have a good local Vietnamese supermarket, you can even try the traditional red tilapia. Whichever you choose, I highly recommend serving it with a side of rice and a light vegetable stir-fry or salad.

Mix all the marinade ingredients together in a bowl, then rub evenly over the hake fillets. Cover and put in the fridge for 1 hour to allow the flavours to soak in, bringing them out to room temperature 30 minutes before cooking.

Add the oil to a frying pan and bring to a low heat. Sprinkle the cornflour (cornstarch) evenly across both sides of the hake fillets, then place them immediately in the pan. Keep at a low heat and fry for 5 minutes, turning over halfway through.

Cover with a lid and cook for a further 2 minutes, then remove the lid and cook for 1 more minute. Use a fork to check if the fillets are ready: if it pulls out easily and the meat is white, it's ready; if not, then cook for a further minute and repeat the test.

Remove the fish from the pan and, leaving the pan over a low heat, throw in the Thai basil leaves for 10–15 seconds, depending on the size of the leaves. Serve the hake with the fried leaves and spring onions (scallions), as well as jasmine rice and chilli oil, if using.

Sautéed Baby Squid and Pineapple

SERVES 4

COOKING TIME: 20 MINUTES

400g (14oz) baby squid rings, cleaned (defrosted, if frozen)

1 tbsp vegetable oil

2 garlic cloves, minced

3 tsp sugar

2 tomatoes, deseeded and diced

½ small pineapple, peeled and diced

1 tbsp sesame oil

1 tsp salt

2 tsp fish sauce

2 spring onions (scallions), finely chopped

5 Thai basil stems, leaves picked

1 red chilli, sliced

2 tsp crispy fried shallots (store-bought or see page 184)

Pineapples are grown all over the Mekong Delta and, as a result, are unsurprisingly popular in my home region; they are often eaten as a snack with chilli salt or mixed into dipping sauces, and are also included as the hero ingredient in traditional seafood stir-fries.

This is a very simple recipe that really showcases the beautiful flavours that pineapple brings to a dish, providing both a sweet and sour note and balancing out the fish sauce.

Place the squid rings in a bowl, pour over boiling water to cover, then drain immediately.

Add the oil to a frying pan and bring to a medium heat. Throw in the garlic and toss for 5–10 seconds, then add the squid rings. Sprinkle over the sugar and toss for 2 minutes to char. Once the squid has turned a little brown and started to caramelize around the edges, take off the heat and remove to bowl.

In the same pan, add the tomatoes, pineapple, sesame oil, salt and fish sauce, then leave to simmer for 1 minute. Add the squid back in with the spring onions (scallions) and toss for a further minute, ensuring that the sauce is mixed evenly around the rings.

Tip into a bowl, sprinkle over the Thai basil, chilli and crispy fried shallots and serve with rice or noodles, or with a crusty bread roll to soak up all that amazing sauce.

Steamed Cod fillet with Prawns

SERVES 4

COOKING TIME: 30 MINUTES

1 tsp vegetable oil

2 garlic cloves, minced

150g (5oz) raw king prawns (shrimp), peeled, deveined and minced

1 red onion, diced

1 tsp salt

2 skinless cod fillets, each 250–280g (9–10oz)

2 thumb-sized pieces of fresh ginger, cut into thin matchsticks

2 spring onions (scallions), cut into thin matchsticks and soaked in cold (tap) water to curl, then drained

1 lime, sliced into thin rounds

1 red chilli, cut into thin matchsticks

1 tsp crispy fried shallots (store-bought or see page 184)

Pinch of crushed black peppercorns

4 coriander (cilantro) stems

FOR THE SAUCE

4 tbsp light soy sauce

1 tbsp sugar

3 tbsp sesame oil

1 tsp garlic paste

1 tsp lemongrass paste

Like many of the best dishes, this recipe came about by chance. I had leftover minced prawns (shrimp) in the fridge from making soup, so I threw them in with the fish I was steaming for lunch and this was the result. Tasty and quick, this is a real winner.

Add the oil to a frying pan and bring to a high heat. Add the garlic and toss for 5–10 seconds until it browns. Add the minced prawns (shrimp) and red onion and fry for a further 1–2 minutes until the prawns are cooked, then take off the heat and set aside.

Set up your steamer over a high heat and bring to boiling point. If you don't have a steamer, take your largest saucepan with a lid, or a small stockpot, and place a heatproof bowl upside down on the bottom. Fill the pan with water to just below the top of the bowl, then place a second bowl, the correct way up, securely on top of the first. Put the lid on and you have a working steamer!

Rub ½ teaspoon of salt into each cod fillet and then cover with the lid and steam for 6–7 minutes until just cooked through, or longer for thicker fillets. Test it's ready by poking the middle with a fork; if it slides in easily and the flesh is fully white, then it's ready.

Place the prawn mixture on top of the cod, cover with the lid and take off the heat.

Add all the sauce ingredients to a small saucepan and slowly stir while bringing to a medium heat.

Remove the fish from the steamer, keeping it on the same hot plate or bowl, if possible, to avoid breaking up the fish. Place the ginger, spring onions (scallions), lime and chilli on the fillets, pour over the sauce and sprinkle on the crispy fried shallots and black pepper. Lastly, add a stem or 2 of coriander (cilantro) and serve with jasmine rice or a side of vegetables.

Sticky Salmon Fillet in a Ginger Soy Glaze

SERVES 2

COOKING TIME: 25 MINUTES

2 sockeye salmon fillets (or regular salmon if not available), each about 180g (6½oz), skin on

½ tsp salt

4 tbsp vegetable oil

3 leeks, halved

30g (1oz) fresh ginger, half thinly sliced and half minced

15g (½oz) curly parsley leaves

2 tbsp light soy sauce

4 tbsp sweet chilli sauce

2 tbsp fish sauce

2 tbsp tamarind paste

When it comes to food, I'm a huge fan of anything with 'sticky' in the title and I wanted to create that wonderful quality here, but in a slightly more subtle way, so that it could be enjoyed with a delicately flavoured ingredient like fish. This recipe combines my love for sticky sauce with wonderful salmon; hopefully you enjoy the combination as much as I do.

Preheat the oven to 170°C/340°F/Gas 4. Pat the salmon dry and rub the salt into the skin.

Add 1 tablespoon of the oil to an ovenproof frying pan and bring to a medium heat. Place the salmon fillets skin-side down in the pan and cook for 4–5 minutes, until the skin is crispy. Transfer to the oven and bake for 3 minutes, then take out and set aside to rest.

Using the same pan, char the baby leeks over a high heat for about 2 minutes on each side, then set aside.

Add 2 tablespoons of the oil to a small saucepan and bring to a medium heat. Fry the sliced ginger and the parsley for 3–4 minutes until crispy. Set aside on paper towels to soak up any excess oil.

Add the remaining tablespoon of oil to the same pan with the minced ginger. Cook for 30 seconds then add the soy sauce, sweet chilli sauce, fish sauce and tamarind paste. Stir together well and leave on the heat for a further 3–4 minutes. Once it has reached a thick consistency and you start to see bubbles, remove from the heat.

Serve the salmon and leeks with the sliced ginger, then pour over the sauce. Garnish with the crispy parsley and enjoy with some fluffy jasmine rice, if you like.

Turmeric and Chilli Honey Cod Nuggets

SERVES 2

COOKING TIME: 25 MINUTES

240g (9oz) skinless cod fillets, roughly chopped

2 tsp ground turmeric

1 tbsp cornflour (cornstarch)

1 tsp salt

1 lime, halved

2 tbsp vegetable oil

4 garlic cloves, minced

10g (⅓oz) fresh ginger, cut into thin matchsticks

8 spring onions (scallions), chopped into 2.5cm (1in) lengths

20g (¾oz) dill, roughly chopped

5 red shallots, thinly sliced lengthways

5g (⅕oz) roasted unsalted peanuts, crushed

1 tbsp crispy fried shallots (store-bought or see page 184)

2 tsp chilli-infused honey, or regular if you prefer

This recipe is inspired by the classic northern Vietnamese dish, Chả Cá Thăng Long. I have played around with it a little by adding a touch of southern sweetness and a little bit of midlands spice. While I love the original dish, I couldn't resist the balance created by fusing all three regions together. I hope you enjoy it too.

Put the cod into a mixing bowl and add the turmeric, cornflour (cornstarch) and salt. Mix, ensuring that all the pieces are coated evenly.

Lightly char the lime halves in a dry frying pan over a medium heat, then remove from the pan and set aside.

Add 1 tablespoon of the oil to the pan and, one by one, add the pieces of cod to the hot oil. Cook for 2 minutes then flip each piece over and cook for a further 2 minutes until the edges are crispy and golden. Leave for a further 30 seconds if needed to achieve the colour, then remove from the heat and transfer to a plate.

Using the same pan, add the remaining tablespoon of oil and increase to a high heat. Add the garlic and ginger and toss for 5 seconds, then add the spring onions (scallions), dill and shallots and toss for a further 30 seconds.

Throw the fish nuggets back in and toss for a final 30 seconds, then tip out onto a plate. To dress, sprinkle over the peanuts and crispy fried shallots, then drizzle over the honey and squeeze the lime halves over to finish. Serve with jasmine rice.

ON THE BBQ

Playing with Fire

Cooking with fire plays a huge part in the Vietnamese street food scene. Among the hustle and bustle of the vibrant markets, this cooking technique has brought us many amazing dishes that are, by design, too irresistible to walk by. From mouthwatering Bún Chả meatballs on the streets of Hanoi, to the succulent Nem Nướng skewers in the village markets of the Mekong Delta, and all the sizzling seafood and barbecued meats in-between.

These already tasty treats are made even more enticing by watching them cook over a naked flame. The drama, the heat, the charred flavour that we all love – and nothing beats watching a seasoned chef cook your meal right in front of your eyes!

I was introduced to cooking over coals at an exceptionally early age, and still to this day I love the theatre of it. Going back to a time when I was arguably a little too young to be playing with fire, our daily routine involved mum setting a small fire in front of our home early each morning, before heading off to work. We would patiently wait until the flame had burnt out, leaving a steady red-hot fire pit. A basket of sweetcorn cobs or sweet potatoes sat pre-prepared on the side for my sister and me to sell throughout the day. First, we'd lay on a row of sweetcorn with its gorgeous green husk still on. I loved watching that layer slowly burn off, knowing that when it did the sweetcorn was ready to serve.

From those early days in my life, I have always had a fascination with cooking using fire, and have spent many happy days tinkering with recipes and playing with sauces in the hope of achieving that perfect result from the process. In this chapter I share some of my favourites. I hope that you get as much enjoyment from them as I have.

Bánh Mì-inspired Brioche Burgers

SERVES 4

COOKING TIME: 15 MINUTES

4 beef burger patties, each 170g (6oz), at room temperature

4 slices of smoked cheese

4 tsp butter

4 brioche buns

80g (3oz) coarse pork or chicken pâté

80g (3oz) carrot and daikon pickle (see page 180)

4 tbsp chilli pepper mayo (see page 179), or regular mayo

2 red chillies, sliced

½ cucumber, sliced into rounds

2 spring onions (scallions), cut into thin matchsticks

20g (¾oz) coriander (cilantro), roughly torn

2 red onions, sliced lengthways

20g (¾oz) mint, leaves picked

Inspired by the most famous street food dish of Vietnam, the key to any good Bánh Mì is the complexity of textures and flavours. Here, faithfully recreated as a burger, rather than the traditional crusty baguette!

Light your BBQ (grill). When ready, sear the burgers on the grill for 2½ minutes each side for medium, adding another minute per side if you prefer well done. (Alternatively, sear them in a frying pan on your stove; the timings are the same, just add 1 teaspoon of vegetable oil per burger.) Add a cheese slice 30 seconds before the completion of the second side and cover the patty with a lid to melt the cheese. If you don't have a burger lid you can simply hold a small frying pan over for the short time it needs. Remove the burger and set aside.

Lightly butter the buns, then place them on the grill, buttered side down, for 15 seconds.

Now for the fun part... it's time to build your burger!

Spread the pâté on the bottom of each bun, then add a beef patty. Next add the pickle and a dollop of the mayo. Place the sliced chillies, cucumber, spring onions (scallions), coriander (cilantro), red onions and mint on top, then add the top bun and your burger is ready to serve!

VARIATIONS
You can replace the beef in this recipe with chicken, vegetables or cold meats. All options work wonderfully and it's good to have a nice variety for your guests to enjoy!

Chilli and Honey Grilled Pineapple

SERVES 4

COOKING TIME: 20 MINUTES

1 large ripe pineapple

a small handful of coriander (cilantro) and mint leaves, finely chopped, plus a few extra stalks for serving

FOR THE GLAZE

1 red chilli, minced

Juice of 1 lime

4 tsp fish sauce

200g (7oz) butter

3 tbsp honey

Pineapple is the perfect balance of sweet and sour, which makes it a useful ingredient in Vietnamese cuisine. I use it as often as I can for salads, soups, stir-fries or like this, as the hero of the dish. This recipe is as simple as it is delicious. A celebration of the pineapple's uniquely balanced flavours and a perfect accompaniment to your summer BBQ. To make it vegetarian, simply swap the fish sauce for soy sauce.

Light your BBQ (grill) and soak 8 wooden bamboo skewers in cold water for 5 minutes. Cut the pineapple lengthways into 8 pieces.

When the BBQ is ready, push the skewers into the pineapple wedges, far enough in to be secure, leaving enough protruding out to manoeuvre them safely on the grill.

Put all the glaze ingredients into a small pan over a low heat. When the butter has fully melted, stir the glaze together, then remove from the heat and set aside.

Using a brush, coat the pineapple wedges in the glaze and grill for 3–4 minutes on each side (depending on size), or until dark and charred around the edges.

Remove from the BBQ and sprinkle over the coriander (cilantro) and mint to serve.

Grilled Aubergine with a Mint Glaze

SERVES 4

COOKING TIME: 40 MINUTES

4 aubergines (eggplants)

20g (¾oz) coriander (cilantro), roughly chopped, plus a few extra leaves for serving

20g (¾oz) mint, leaves picked, plus extra for serving

2 garlic cloves, roughly chopped

15ml (1 tbsp) lime juice or white wine vinegar

50ml (3½ tbsp) sesame oil

Pinch of salt

Pinch of sugar

2 tsp crushed black peppercorns

4 spring onions (scallions), finely chopped

400ml (14fl oz) nước chấm fish sauce (see page 182)

4 tsp crispy fried shallots (store-bought or see page 184)

There are many ways to cook aubergine (eggplant), but for me nothing quite beats the charred flavour of cooking it over fire. Whether on a fancy BBQ or the flames of your stove, the wonderful smoky taste complements Vietnamese fish sauce and aubergine perfectly.

Switch the fish sauce for soy sauce and this becomes a perfect vegan summer dish.

Light your BBQ (grill) and when ready, place the aubergines (eggplants) on the grill. Cook for 15–20 minutes, depending on size, turning every 5 minutes to ensure an even cook, until soft to the touch with the skin burnt and flaky. Remove from the heat, leave to cool for 10 minutes, then carefully peel the skin off.

While the aubergines are cooling, make the dressing. Put the coriander (cilantro), mint, garlic and lime juice in a food processor or blender and blitz for 3–5 seconds. Pour into a bowl, then add the sesame oil, salt, sugar and black pepper. Mix everything together and set aside.

Put the aubergines on your serving plate and firmly run a fork down the length of each one a few times. You're aiming to make deep enough grooves that the dressing can fully soak in.

Sprinkle over the spring onions (scallions), pour on the nước chấm fish sauce, then drizzle the mint and coriander dressing on top. Serve topped with the crispy fried shallots and some extra herbs, if you like.

Grilled Mackerel with a Pear, Red Chicory and Rocket Salad

SERVES 4

COOKING TIME: 10 MINUTES,
PLUS CHILLING

4 fresh mackerel fillets

2 tsp sesame oil

2 pinches of salt

2 blush pears, thinly sliced

2 red chicory (endive) heads,
  leaves roughly torn

100g (3½oz) rocket (arugula)
  leaves

200ml (7fl oz) tamarind fish sauce
  (see page 181)

4 tsp crispy fried shallots
  (store-bought or see page 184)

1 lemon, cut into wedges

Much of Vietnamese cuisine is both healthy and delicious; even the special once-a-year meals are a balanced affair, with at least a couple of your five-a-day included. This recipe is no exception – it's packed full of nutrition and will blow you away when you taste it. Oh, and it comes together in no time at all. What more could you want from your dinner? Pictured on page 108.

Rub the mackerel fillets evenly with the sesame oil and salt, then place in the fridge for at least 30 minutes, but no longer than 3 hours or they will start to dry out. Remove from the fridge and let the fish get to room temperature 30 minutes before cooking.

Light your BBQ (grill). When ready, place the fillets on the grill and cook for 5 minutes, turning halfway.

Meanwhile, toss the pears, chicory (endive) and rocket (arugula) together in a mixing bowl, and dress with the tamarind fish sauce to taste.

Serve the mackerel and salad, then sprinkle with the crispy fried shallots and serve with a wedge of lemon.

Grilled Chilli Oysters

SERVES 4

COOKING TIME: 15 MINUTES

12 oysters, shucked and cleaned
(get your fishmonger to do this),
shells reserved

100g (3½oz) salmon roe (optional)

FOR THE SAUCE

2 tbsp fish sauce

6 tbsp sweet chilli sauce

6 tbsp warm water

2 tbsp lime juice or rice wine
vinegar

3 red chillies, minced

4 garlic cloves, minced

5g (⅕oz) chives, finely chopped

5g (⅕oz) coriander (cilantro),
finely chopped

Invite your friends over, chill a bottle of something nice, fire up the BBQ and enjoy these lusciously indulgent oysters! Pictured on page 109.

Light your BBQ (grill).

Put the fish sauce, sweet chilli sauce, warm water, lime juice, chilli and garlic in a bowl and mix together well. Add the chives and coriander (cilantro) and set aside.

When the BBQ is ready, lay your oysters (in their shells) on the grill and cook for 40 seconds. Add a teaspoon of the sauce to each oyster shell and cook for a further 15–20 seconds until you see it sizzling. Take straight from the grill to a serving plate and add a teaspoon of roe to each to garnish, if using.

Warning: these will disappear faster than you expect, so make sure to have a sneaky taste before serving your guests!

Jumbo Red Curry Tiger Prawns

SERVES 6

COOKING TIME: 10 MINUTES, PLUS CHILLING

6 shell-on raw jumbo tiger prawns (shrimp) or raw king prawns

7 tsp red curry paste

50g (1¾oz) butter

6 tsp garlic paste

20g (¾oz) chives, finely chopped

2 tbsp crispy fried shallots (store-bought or see page 184)

2 lemons, cut into wedges

If you like big prawns with big flavours, then you will love this recipe. Butterflying the prawns sounds more complicated than it is – and very little effort is required, so there's more time for you to stand back and watch the fire at work. Just make sure not to burn the prawns.

Butterfly the prawns (shrimp) by lying them flat with the belly facing up, then cut down the centre from the head to the tail. You are aiming to cut all the way through the meat without damaging the shell on the back. Spread each prawn wide, flatten out, and devein by removing the black line that runs down the back, using your knife. If using raw king prawns, butterflying is optional, but do remove the black line.

Rub 1 teaspoon of red curry paste onto the meat of each prawn and put in the fridge for at least 30 minutes to marinate, but no more than 3 hours or they will start to dry out. Remove from the fridge and let them get to room temperature for 30 minutes before cooking.

Light your BBQ (grill).

Add the butter, garlic paste and remaining teaspoon of red curry paste to a small pan and bring to a medium heat. Once the butter has melted, add the chives and take off the heat.

When the BBQ is ready, place the prawns on the grill and cook for 2–3 minutes each side or 1–2 minutes if using raw king prawns.

Serve the prawns, pour over the sauce and garnish with a sprinkling of crispy fried shallots and a squeeze of lemon.

Lemongrass and Honey Pork Skewers

MAKES 12

COOKING TIME: 40 MINUTES, PLUS MARINATING

500g (1lb 2oz) pork belly

200ml (7fl oz) lemongrass chilli oil (see page 180)

40g (1½oz) roasted unsalted peanuts, roughly crushed in a pestle and mortar

4 tsp crispy fried shallots (store-bought or see page 184)

FOR THE MARINADE

2 tbsp red chilli paste

2 tbsp garlic paste

2 tbsp lemongrass paste

2 tbsp fish sauce

6 tbsp oyster sauce

3 chicken stock cubes, crumbled

5 tbsp sesame oil

4 tbsp honey

1 tbsp ground black pepper

TO SERVE

400g (14oz) carrot and daikon pickle (see page 180), optional

200ml (7fl oz) nước chấm fish sauce (see page 182)

Like most people, I grew up thinking that my mum was the best cook in the world. OK, maybe not the best, but in the top 10 for sure. Now, as a grown-up and a mother myself, I've come to realize that I was right all along, she is. Certainly for traditional Vietnamese food anyway.

A few years ago, I was in Ho Chi Minh City with my husband, and we saw a lady with a wooden trolley selling lemongrass pork skewers. One item on the menu, take it or leave it. We ordered a couple and, after that first bite, I was hooked. I'd had my mum's version and it's amazing, but this was on a whole other level. A recipe mastered over generations by a family and their one-dish mobile restaurant. We spent quite some time down that little alleyway happily devouring skewer after skewer.

So, here's my mum's recipe for these unforgettable skewers, truly delicious and only second to one.

Cut the pork belly lengthways into strips, then cut the strips across into thin slices. Make sure they are as even in thickness as possible so cooking time on the fire will be the same.

Put all the marinade ingredients in a large bowl and mix together well. Add the pork slices, then gently and evenly cover in the marinade. Put into the fridge for 3 hours to marinate, or ideally overnight for best results.

RECIPE CONTINUES

Light your BBQ (grill) and soak 12 bamboo skewers, 18cm (7in) long, in cold water for 5 minutes.

One at a time, add the pork slices to the skewers, weaving them on and packing them down the skewer as you go. I recommend doing this with a chatty friend or with some good music in the background.

When the BBQ is ready, put the skewers on the grill and cook for 15–20 minutes, turning them halfway.

Serve the skewers, drizzle over the lemongrass chilli oil, then sprinkle the peanuts and crispy fried shallots on top.

Serve with the carrot and daikon pickle and a bowl of nước chấm fish sauce on the side.

Turmeric Oyster and Shiitake Mushroom Skewers

SERVES 4

COOKING TIME: 15 MINUTES

200g (7oz) oyster mushrooms

200g (7oz) king oyster mushrooms

200g (7oz) fresh shiitake mushrooms

6 spring onions (scallions), stems chopped into 2.5cm (1in) pieces, bulbs halved

FOR THE GLAZE

2 tsp ground turmeric

5 tbsp sesame oil

1 chicken stock cube, crumbled

2 tsp oyster sauce

2 tsp garlic paste

100g (3½oz) butter

20g (¾oz) chives, finely chopped

There's something that feels adventurous about eating exotic mushrooms. Maybe it's something to do with their almost unearthly beauty, or maybe it's the unique texture. Either way, I love them and the subtle yet distinctive flavour they add to a dish. From the humble button mushroom to its cousin the shiitake, all types of fungi are welcome at my party.

This is a simple recipe that celebrates the mushroom as the hero ingredient that it deserves to be. Pictured on page 113.

Light your BBQ (grill) and soak 8 bamboo skewers in cold water for 5 minutes.

Put all the glaze ingredients into a small pan and place over a low heat until the butter melts. Give it a quick stir, remove from the heat and leave to cool.

Cut the mushrooms as needed to create similar size pieces from all. Slide onto the skewers, alternating the variety as you go and adding spring onion (scallion) pieces in between.

When the BBQ is ready, rub the glaze evenly over the skewers and grill for 3–5 minutes on each side, turning them often to keep the char even. You are aiming for tender and juicy mushrooms that have a bouncy texture on the bite.

You can serve these skewers as they are or with any of the dipping sauces on pages 179–184. For a vegan-friendly option, try them with the hoisin dipping sauce on page 134.

Prawn-stuffed Piccerella Peppers

SERVES 2–3 AS A SNACK

COOKING TIME: 25 MINUTES

5–6 Piccerella peppers, about 150g (5oz) in total, halved and deseeded

FOR THE PRAWN MIXTURE

250–300g (9–10½oz) raw king prawns (shrimp), peeled and deveined

2 spring onions (scallions), roughly chopped

½ tsp salt

½ tsp ground black pepper

½ tsp sugar

3 tsp sesame oil

FOR THE GLAZE

50ml (3½ tbsp) light soy sauce

50ml (3½ tbsp) vegetable oil

Juice of ½ lime

5 tsp sugar

2 tsp sweet chilli sauce

This is the perfect summer recipe. They look amazing, and they taste even better thanks to the lovely sweetness of the peppers. If you prefer, you can also bake these in an oven preheated to 200°C/400°F/Gas 6 for 12–15 minutes. This recipe also works really well with Portobello mushrooms and large, juicy tomatoes, if you can't get hold of Piccerella peppers – you'll just need to adjust the timings.

Light your BBQ (grill).

Add all the prawn (shrimp) mixture ingredients to a blender or food processor and blitz for 10–15 seconds, making sure to keep the chunks relatively big.

Add the glaze ingredients to a small pan and bring to the boil over a low heat. Take off the heat as soon as the sugar has dissolved. At this point you should see a slight thickening of the sauce and bubbles forming on the surface. Set aside.

Fill the peppers with the prawn mixture and cook on the grill, covered with a BBQ lid or small pan, for 6–8 minutes, depending on size. (See the introduction if you would prefer to cook these in the oven.)

Drizzle the glaze over the prawn-stuffed peppers when serving or simply use as a dip.

Shrimp Floss Butter Corn on the Cob

SERVES 4

COOKING TIME: 20 MINUTES

4 sweetcorn cobs, husks removed

20g (¾oz) butter

2 tbsp sesame oil

4 spring onions (scallions), finely chopped

1 tsp chilli powder

100g (3½oz) dried shrimp, blitzed to a floss

This is not just any corn on the cob! Onion oil with salt is the traditional dressing for sweetcorn in Vietnam and is how I've eaten BBQ sweetcorn for most of my life. This is essentially doing the same job as butter, adding a saltiness and an oily texture that works so well with sweetcorn. It doesn't quite have the same rich and decadent flavour as butter, though, so I also add moreish shrimp floss to maximize the umami flavours and help take your corn to a new level.

Light your BBQ (grill).

When the BBQ is ready, put the cobs on the grill and cook for 10–15 minutes, turning frequently to keep the charring even.

While they're cooking, set up a small saucepan on the grill and add the butter, sesame oil and spring onions (scallions). Bring to a medium heat until the butter has melted, then stir together, remove from the heat and set aside.

Add the chilli powder to the shrimp floss and mix until combined.

When the sweetcorn is ready, spoon over the melted butter and spring onions and sprinkle over the chilli shrimp floss.

Spicy Wraps with Pineapple Fish Sauce

MAKES 8

COOKING TIME: 30 MINUTES, PLUS CHILLING

200g (7oz) vermicelli rice noodles

48 perilla leaves or shiso (or use collard greens, see note opposite)

2 red onions, sliced into thin wedges

4 baby gem lettuce, leaves separated

20g (¾oz) mint, leaves picked

20g (¾oz) coriander (cilantro) stems, halved

2 red chillies, thinly sliced

500ml (17fl oz/generous 2 cups) pineapple fish sauce (see page 181), to serve

FOR THE FILLING

500g (1lb 2oz) minced (ground) beef

4 spring onions (scallions), finely chopped

4 tsp lemongrass paste

4 tsp garlic paste

2 tsp chilli paste

1 tsp light soy sauce

1 tsp oyster sauce

2 tsp fish sauce

2 tbsp sesame oil

3 tsp sugar

3 tsp ground black pepper

This is inspired by the traditional Bò Lá Lốt, made using Lá Lốt, or betel leaves, which are delicious but can be especially difficult to source outside of Vietnam. I originally created this alternative using perilla leaves for my restaurant menu. Available in most East and Southeast Asian stores and online, perilla is far easier to find and works beautifully in this recipe.

This is a winning dish whatever the weather, so put up your umbrella and fire up that BBQ! Taking it indoors will still be delicious, but on the fire is where it's meant to be; that charred flavour on the leaves is too good to miss out on.

For such a show-off dish, these little flavour bombs are surprisingly easy to make, and also really fun to eat. Like summer rolls, they have a wonderful ability to bring your diners together. Just put the lettuce, noodles and herbs in the middle of the table and let everyone wrap their own.

Pictured on page 122.

Put all the filling ingredients into a bowl and, using your hands, mix together well. Leave in the fridge for an hour, then remove and allow to come to room temperature 30 minutes before cooking.

Light your BBQ (grill).

Cook the noodles according to the packet instructions, then drain and set aside.

Place a perilla leaf on a board, shiny-side down with the stem pointing towards you. Put a tablespoon of the filling mixture on the base of the leaf, just above the stem, adjusting the amount depending on the size of the leaf. Add a wedge of red onion on top, pressing firmly into the mixture, then roll the leaf into a cylinder, starting from the stem. Place the roll seam-down so it stays in shape, then repeat 5 times so you have 6 filled leaves.

Soak 8 bamboo skewers, 18cm (7in), in cold water for 5 minutes before use. Carefully slide all 6 rolls onto a skewer, making sure that the tips of the end pieces are facing inwards so they're secure when cooking. See the picture overleaf.

Repeat the process for the remaining 7 skewers, then when the BBQ is ready, place the skewers on the grill and cook for 2 minutes on each side.

To serve, lay a lettuce leaf on your plate and add some noodles, mint, coriander (cilantro), chilli and finally a stuffed perilla.

Make sure you have a bowl of pineapple fish sauce nearby so you're ready to dip.

NOTE
If you can't source perilla or shiso leaves, collard greens will give different but still nice results. To use them, wash the leaves, cut each in half lengthways as close to the stem as possible, discarding the stem, then roll as directed above.

WEEKENDS & PARTIES

Feeding a Crowd

Good friends and great food are the perfect combination to get your weekend started! I am a firm believer that a full belly produces the best laughter, and a conversation held against a background of appreciative 'mmms' and 'ahhhs' is a very satisfying one to be a part of.

I noticed soon after arriving in London that fun is mainly saved up for the weekends. Back in my village in Vietnam, every day was very similar to the last. The market was still open with the sellers all in their regular positions from very early in the morning. All my chores and tasks were the same. The only difference being that there was no school. In England, though, the weekend was something to be excited about. It seemed there was a shared anticipation of the coming weekend. It felt to me like a beautiful weekly tradition, and I was sold on it immediately. As an immigrant in a new culture, I loved feeling part of something. I mainly liked it though as my weekend plans always involved eating! Phở was often on the menu, or another favourite deemed too laborious for a weekday meal, and as the Viet community would gather each weekend, all manner of party dishes could be eagerly anticipated as well.

Preparation for those gatherings back then consisted of long hours trekking around London with mum, hunting down available Vietnamese ingredients, travelling to several different locations across the city by bus, just to gather the herbs and spices needed to put on a pot of Phở. Mum was often forced to get creative with her recipes as she had to replace the unavailable ingredients, but that never diminished the deliciousness! When these gatherings coincided with a celebration day, then the feast would really get serious. I think being so far from home both culturally and geographically meant that a huge importance was placed on community, and especially the food.

From the arrival of the guests until the minute they left, mum would be focused on being the perfect host, making sure everyone was well fed, multiple times, and therefore happy. They always were, and so was she when she saw how much joy her food had brought them. I remember seeing how exhausted she was after a party; seeing the tiredness behind the happy smile. I thought that it was just meant to be that way, as that is how I was taught to host and to show love to family and friends. That is my experience of my culture.

As tends to happen, as I grew up I slowly became my mum, taking on many of the traits and habits that I swore I never would – and this was one. I would only feel satisfied if my friends were rolling home at the end of an evening with a full belly. The exhaustion of hosting was perfectly balanced by the joy that feeding friends would bring me. Now I have learned to maximize these moments of friendship and adapt the food to accommodate them. Not the other way round! I have made an effort to adjust my ways so there is more of a healthy balance when entertaining and hosting. However, as much as I have learned and grown, I cannot change the fact that I am at heart a Viet girl from the Mekong Delta. The food is, and always will be, vitally important.

If I could go back in time and talk to my younger mum, I would tell her a good dish doesn't have to be complicated. It doesn't have to be something that only she is able to make. That her friends will possibly have even more fun if they aren't completely full and would also feel joy seeing her enjoy herself at the party.

When friends and family arrive, I want to be there in the moment with them, enjoying the food and the company – time we cannot take back once it's gone. And now that my hairs are starting to grey, I find myself really treasuring the moments I get to share with the people I love.

You'll find that some of the ingredients in this chapter are a little more special, intended as treats for yourself and your guests, and are central to these guaranteed crowd-pleasers. All in all, these are fun dishes to share that are uncomplicated to prepare and perfect for all types of hosts.

Rice Paper Dumplings

This is a great recipe for a gathering of foodie friends who like to cook together and have a chat at the same time.

MAKES 24

COOKING TIME: 50 MINUTES,
PLUS CHILLING

24 garlic chives (or long spring
onion/scallion stems, halved
lengthways)

6 x 22cm (8½in) squares of rice
paper, each cut into quarters

2 egg yolks, lightly beaten

About 500ml (17fl oz/generous
2 cups) vegetable oil

200ml (7fl oz) chilli pepper mayo
(see page 179) or regular mayo

FOR THE FILLING

100g (3½oz) dried shiitake
mushrooms

100g (3½oz) garlic chives (or use
regular chives), chopped

300g (10½oz) raw king prawns
(shrimp), peeled and deveined

100g (3½oz) fine asparagus
spears, finely chopped

2 pinches of salt

2 tsp sugar

2 tsp ground black pepper

4 tsp sesame oil

1 tsp fish sauce

1 tsp light soy sauce

2 chicken stock cubes, crumbled

2 spring onions (scallions),
roughly chopped

3 tsp cornflour (cornstarch)

Put the dried shiitake mushrooms into a heatproof bowl, add boiling water to cover and leave for 15 minutes to soak. Drain, squeeze dry and finely chop.

If using garlic chives, cut off the white root of the 24, then put into a bowl, cover in boiling water and leave to soak for 1 minute, then drain and set aside to dry.

Put all the filling ingredients, including the soaked mushrooms, into a food processor and blitz for 7–8 seconds, ensuring that the texture remains lumpy rather than reducing to a paste. Chill in the fridge for 1–3 hours.

Half-fill a large bowl with warm water. Dip a piece of paper towel in the water and make a single wipe across both sides of a rice paper quarter. Wait for 10–15 seconds until it is soft enough to bend, then add a tablespoon of filling to the centre of the paper.

Dip your index finger into the beaten egg yolk and wipe it in a thick line along each outer edge of the paper. Now lift two opposing corners of paper up over the filling and squeeze together at the top. Repeat with the other two corners, squeezing all 4 together at the neck to roughly close. Tightly pinch the neck and twist the dumpling round to firmly close, then use a chive to tie a cute knot. You are aiming for almost too pretty to eat, but way too delicious not to! Repeat with the remaining squares of rice paper and filling.

Pour enough oil into a small, heavy-based saucepan to partially submerge the dumplings, then bring to 170°C (340°F). An easy way to tell when the oil is ready is by placing a wooden chopstick into the oil and waiting until bubbles start to form around it on the surface of the oil. In batches of 3 or 4, carefully place the dumplings in the hot oil one at a time, making sure they aren't touching or they will stick and tear. Shallow-fry for 2 minutes, then remove with a slotted spoon onto paper towels to drain.

Serve with a bowl of chilli pepper mayo for dipping, then tuck in!

Coconut and Lemongrass Langoustines

SERVES 4

COOKING TIME: 20 MINUTES

1 tbsp vegetable oil

4 lemongrass stalks, crushed

5g (⅕oz) fresh ginger, sliced

3 red shallots, peeled and halved

6 fresh lime leaves

1 lime, halved

20g (¾oz) butter

330ml (11fl oz) coconut water

100ml (3½fl oz) white wine

½ tsp salt

2 tbsp sugar

2 tbsp fish sauce

2 chicken stock cubes, crumbled

1kg (2lb 3oz) medium langoustines
(about 20), halved

TO SERVE

3 tbsp spring onion oil
(see page 179)

1 tbsp crispy fried shallots
(store-bought or see page 184)

10g (⅓oz) Vietnamese mint or
Thai basil, leaves picked

1 red chilli, sliced

Everything can be made a little sweeter with coconut water. I'm from the Mekong Delta, an area that is abundant with coconuts, so much so they are often used instead of water in cooking – this might explain why southern Vietnamese often enjoy much sweeter dishes than in the rest of the country. Here I have paired it with luscious langoustines. Prawns, mussels, clams and other seafood also work nicely with the coconut and lemongrass, if you can't get hold of langoustines.

Add the oil to a large sauté pan over a high heat. When hot, add the lemongrass, ginger, shallots, lime leaves and lime halves and fry for 3–5 minutes until charred. Remove the lime halves and set aside.

Add the butter, coconut water, wine, salt, sugar, fish sauce and crumbled stock cubes and bring to the boil. When you see bubbles, lay the langoustines in the pan, flesh side up. Cover with a lid and cook for 3–4 minutes, then remove from the heat.

Serve drizzled generously with the spring onion oil, then sprinkle over the crispy fried shallots and dress with the herbs and the chilli. Lastly, squeeze over the reserved charred lime and enjoy!

Pork and Egg
Sticky Rice

SERVES 4

**COOKING TIME: 1½ HOURS,
PLUS MARINATING**

500g (1lb 2oz) pork belly strips
(no skin)

500g (1lb 2oz) uncooked
sticky rice

2 tbsp vegetable oil

330ml (11fl oz) coconut water

2 large eggs, beaten

2 lạp xưởng (Chinese pork
sausage), cut into thin
matchsticks

200g (7oz) carrot and daikon
pickle (see page 180)

4 tbsp nước chấm fish sauce
(see page 182)

4 tbsp spring onion oil
(see page 179)

50g (1¾oz) dried shrimp,
blitzed to a floss

6 tsp crispy fried shallots
(store-bought or see page 184)

When I was younger and saw my mum holding a little green
parcel wrapped with banana leaves, I would get excited – it
would mean either a sweetcorn dessert or this incredible
sticky rice savoury treat. Either way, a win. It was a very rare
treat and only ever a small portion, so I always made sure I
savoured every bite. This is a dish that still makes the child
in me happy and I love sharing that happiness, through this
modern version.

Blitz all the marinade ingredients together in a blender. Pour over
the pork belly strips, rub well, cover and leave in the fridge to
marinate for 24 hours.

Place the sticky rice in a large bowl, add room-temperature water
to cover and soak for 24 hours.

Drain and dry the rice. Set up your steamer on a high heat and
bring to boiling point. If you don't have a steamer, then take your
largest saucepan with a lid, or a small stockpot, and place a bowl
upside down on the bottom. Fill the pan with water to just below
the top of the bowl, then place a second bowl, the correct way
up, securely on top of the first. Put the lid on and you have a
working steamer!

Steam the rice for 35–45 minutes until soft. Take off the heat but
keep the rice covered until serving to avoid it drying out.

FOR THE MARINADE

5 red shallots, peeled

3 garlic cloves, peeled

2 chicken stock cubes, crumbled

3 tsp sriracha chilli sauce

2 tsp brown sugar

2 tsp fish sauce

4 tsp oyster sauce

2 tsp rice wine vinegar

5 tsp sesame oil

2 tsp ground black pepper

While the rice is steaming, heat 1 tablespoon of the vegetable oil in a medium frying pan, add the pork belly strips and cook for 2–3 minutes on high, browning the surfaces and edges. Add the coconut water and simmer for 15–20 minutes until the sauce has caramelized. Remove the pork and set aside.

Heat another ½ tablespoon of oil in a small frying pan. Pour half of the beaten eggs into the pan to make a thin omelette. Remove from the pan and slice into fine strips. Set aside and repeat the process with the other half of the beaten eggs.

Add the remaining ½ tablespoon of oil to the small frying pan, add the strips of sausage and toss for 20–30 seconds. As soon as you see a change in colour to bright red, take off the heat.

Once the pork belly has cooled, it's ready to slice. Traditionally it would be sliced thinly but some days I prefer nice big chunks. It's your choice depending on your mood.

To serve, place a large portion of the sticky rice on your serving plate. Around the rice, add the pork, omelette strips, sausage and carrot and daikon pickle.

For that extra layer of flavour, drizzle the nước chấm fish sauce and spring onion oil generously over the dish, then sprinkle over the shrimp floss and crispy fried shallots to finish.

Confit Duck Lettuce Rolls

SERVES 4

COOKING TIME: 3 HOURS, PLUS SALTING

2 duck legs, each about 200g (7oz)

2 tsp salt

1 litre (2 pints) duck fat (or use vegetable oil)

200g (7oz) vermicelli rice noodles

2 cos lettuce, leaves separated

1 cucumber, cut into thin matchsticks

1 large carrot, cut into thin matchsticks

20g (¾oz) mint leaves

20g (¾oz) Thai basil leaves

15 coriander (cilantro) stems

FOR THE HOISIN DIPPING SAUCE

1 tbsp vegetable oil

2 garlic cloves, minced

1 red chilli, minced

5 tbsp hoisin sauce

3 tbsp peanut butter

5 tbsp water

2 tsp sesame oil

3 tsp rice wine vinegar or lime juice

2 tbsp roasted unsalted peanuts, roughly crushed in a pestle and mortar

These rolls would usually be eaten with whole fried white fish, and in some regions of Vietnam, rice paper would be used for the outer layer. This recipe is far from traditional and takes inspiration and influence from French and Chinese cookery, with the use of confit and hoisin. Confit is a classic French preparation of meat and is not a commonly practised technique in Vietnam. It originated as a method of preserving without the use of refrigeration and involves curing and gently slow cooking the meat. I am still championing the uptake of the process today, though, as it makes the meat so tender that it falls off the bone, yet it's crispy at the same time! This recipe uses this gorgeous meat in a lettuce wrap, turning it into a delicious party treat.

Wipe dry the duck legs with paper towels, rub 1 teaspoon of salt onto each leg and refrigerate for 12–24 hours.

Preheat the oven to 150°C/300°F/Gas 2.

Put the duck legs in a roasting tin, cover with the duck fat and cook in the oven for 2½ hours.

Meanwhile, make the hoisin dipping sauce. Put the oil, garlic and chilli in a small saucepan and toss over a medium heat for 10–15 seconds until brown. Turn to a low heat and add the hoisin sauce, peanut butter, water, sesame oil and rice vinegar. Simmer for 2–3 minutes, slowly stirring continuously, until you see bubbles. Personally, I like the sauce thick but loosen with water to adjust the thickness to your liking.

RECIPE CONTINUES

When the duck is ready, remove it from the fat and place on paper towels to absorb the excess fat. Let it cool for 10 minutes, then tear off the meat into strips.

Cook and drain the vermicelli rice noodles according to the packet instructions.

Place a small handful of vermicelli noodles in a lettuce leaf, then add a generous serving of duck. Place on top some cucumber and carrot, a few mint and Thai basil leaves and a stem of coriander (cilantro). Pinch the outsides of the leaf together to close and secure with a toothpick. Repeat this process for all of your ingredients.

Plate the lettuce rolls, sprinkle the crushed roasted peanuts on top of the hoisin dipping sauce and serve it alongside the rolls.

TIP
Cool down the leftover duck fat and remove the jelly – the oil left underneath is really flavoursome and delicious for roasting, or it can be reused next time you confit.

Prawn and Kohlrabi Tofu Parcels

MAKES 20

COOKING TIME: 30 MINUTES

10 tofu skin (bean curd) sheets

60g (2oz) cornflour (cornstarch)

120ml (4fl oz/½ cup) water

200ml (7fl oz) nước chấm fish
sauce (see page 182), to serve

FOR THE FILLING

500g (1lb 2oz) raw king prawns
(shrimp), peeled, deveined
and minced

1 large carrot, finely diced

1 kohlrabi, peeled and finely diced

2 spring onions (scallions),
finely chopped

1 tsp sugar

1 tsp ground black pepper

½ tsp salt

2 tsp fish sauce

1 chicken stock cube, crumbled

This recipe is inspired by my love of dim sum. I wanted to create a Vietnamese version of this Chinese classic as it's long been one of my 'must haves' when dining out. There are several ways to cook tofu skin (available in East and Southeast Asian stores or online) depending on which region the dish originates from, and this recipe uses my favourite method of steaming. Here, I serve these parcels with Vietnamese fish sauce, but they are perfect sauce-soaking vessels so will work with any number of delicious moreish dips, making them ideal for party bites.

Cut the tofu skin (bean curd) sheets into squares approximately 10cm (4in) in diameter and set aside.

Mix the cornflour (cornstarch) and water together to make a paste and set aside.

Put all the filling ingredients in bowl and mix together.

Take a sheet of tofu skin and brush with the cornflour paste. Place a heaped tablespoon of filling just below the centre of the skin, or a little more if you prefer, then fold the roll like an envelope, bringing the two sides in towards the centre with roughly 3cm (1¼in) folds. Next, fold the top flap down and roll from the bottom, all the way up to the top. Repeat with the remaining tofu sheets, paste and filling.

RECIPE CONTINUES

Set up your steamer on a high heat and bring to the boiling point. If you don't have a steamer, then take your largest saucepan with a lid, or a small stockpot, and place a bowl upside down on the bottom. Fill the pan with water to just below the top of the bowl, then place a second bowl, the correct way up, securely on top of the first. Put the lid on and you have a working steamer.

Place the parcels in the steamer in a single layer and steam for 15–20 minutes.

Just before serving, pan-fry the parcels (or use a little vegetable oil if necessary) over a medium heat, to get that crispy layer. Just 2–3 minutes each side will do the trick, but make sure you keep an eye on them as they will go from not ready to burnt in just a few seconds!

Serve with a bowl of nước chấm fish sauce for dipping.

Pork and Truffle Steamed Rice Rolls

SERVES 4

COOKING TIME: 30 MINUTES

200g (7oz) beansprouts

20 round or square rice paper
sheets, 22cm (8½in)

1 cucumber, cut into thin
matchsticks

20g (¾oz) mint leaves,
finely chopped

20g (¾oz) Thai basil leaves,
finely chopped

300ml (10fl oz/1¼ cups) nước
chấm fish sauce (see page 182)

4 tsp crispy fried shallots
(store-bought or see page 184)

Truffle shavings (optional)

2 tbsp truffle oil

FOR THE FILLING

1 tbsp vegetable oil

500g (1lb 2oz) minced
(ground) pork

200g (7oz) fresh king oyster or
shiitake mushrooms, finely diced

2 medium carrots, finely diced

2 onions, finely diced

1 tsp salt

3 tsp sugar

2 tsp fish sauce

2 tsp ground black pepper

1 tsp oyster sauce

2 tbsp truffle oil

What cannot be improved with truffle? If, like me, you can't think of many good answers to that question, then we can definitely be friends. If you also love Bánh Cuốn rolls, then you have most certainly found yourself on the right page of this book. Here I've used dry rice paper sheets instead of making the traditional-style rice flour batter from scratch, so this comes together in a fraction of the time. Pictured on page 142.

For the filling, add most of the vegetable oil to a large frying pan and bring to a high heat. Add the rest of the filling ingredients and toss together for 5–8 minutes, stirring to break up any clumps, until light brown. Take off the heat and set aside.

Put the beansprouts into a heatproof bowl, add boiling water to cover for a few seconds, then drain and set aside to dry.

Add a little more vegetable oil to a bowl of water big enough to fit a rice paper. Take a rice paper and soak for 30–45 seconds until soft but not too floppy. Gently shake off as much water as you can, then lay on a clean dish cloth. Place a heaped tablespoon of filling (or a little more if you prefer) just below the centre of the paper, then fold the roll like an envelope, bringing the two sides in towards the centre with roughly 3cm (1¼in) folds. Next, fold the top flap down and roll from the bottom, all the way up to the top. Repeat with the remaining rice papers and filling.

Set up your steamer on a high heat and bring to the boiling point. If you don't have a steamer, then take your largest saucepan with a lid, or a small stockpot, and place a bowl upside down on the bottom. Fill the pan with water to just below the top of the bowl, then place a second bowl, the correct way up, securely on top of the first. Put the lid on and you have a working steamer!

Steam the rolls one layer at a time for 2–3 minutes, until soft.

Plate up the rolls and add the beansprouts, cucumber, mint and Thai basil. Pour on the nước chấm fish sauce and sprinkle on the crispy fried shallots and truffle shavings, if using. Lastly, drizzle the truffle oil over the top and you are ready to serve.

Bánh Patê Sô-inspired Pasties

MAKES 24 MINI PASTIES

COOKING TIME: 1 HOUR

15g (½oz) dried wood ear mushrooms (or use dried porcini or shiitake)

50g (1¾oz) mung bean noodles

2 tbsp vegetable oil

150g (5oz) minced (ground) pork

150g (5oz) raw king prawns (shrimp), peeled, deveined and minced

1 small carrot, finely diced

2 x 320g (11¼oz) puff pastry sheets

1 large egg, separated

FOR THE SEASONING

1 tsp salt

2 tsp sugar

1 chicken stock cube, crumbled

1 tsp crushed black peppercorns

1 tsp fish sauce

2 tsp oyster sauce

This popular Vietnamese puff pastry was created with a heavy French influence back in the 19th century. Pork is the traditional choice of filling but it also works well with beef, or chicken if you want a lighter option. I have added prawns as I love the bouncy texture that they bring to the dish! If you have any leftover filling, it's great added to omelettes or stir-fries.

These are great little treats for party nibbles. Pictured on page 143.

Prepare the wood ear mushrooms and mung bean noodles separately by soaking in boiling water for 4–6 minutes then draining in a sieve for 20 minutes before removing and patting dry with paper towels. Remove to a chopping board, finely chop and set aside.

Add 1 tablespoon of the oil to a large frying pan and bring to a high heat. Add the pork and prawns (shrimp) and cook, stirring to break up any clumps, for 4–6 minutes until the pork is a light brown. Remove, drain and set aside.

In the same pan, add the remaining oil and bring to a high heat. Add the carrot, mushrooms and noodles and cook for 2 minutes, then add the pork and prawns, along with all the seasoning ingredients. Mix everything together well and cook for a further 2 minutes, then take off the heat and leave to cool.

Preheat the oven to 180°C/350°F/Gas 4.

Separate the filling into 24 equal portions.

Cut the pastry into about 5.5cm (2¼in) squares; you will need 2 squares for each pasty, so should have 48 in total. Brush a layer of egg white over half the squares then spoon a ball of filling to the centre of each. Place the second square on top, building a dome around the ball of filling. Press the two squares together then crimp the edges using a fork.

Place the pasties on a lined baking sheet, brush egg yolk across the tops and bake for 25–30 minutes, until golden and cooked.

Bacon and Egg
Bánh Mì-style Croissant

SERVES 2

COOKING TIME: 15 MINUTES

2 tsp vegetable oil

4 slices of streaky bacon

2 eggs

2 croissants

2 tsp coarse pork or chicken pâté

2 tsp mayonnaise

40g (1½oz) carrot and daikon
  pickle (see page 180)

6 coriander (cilantro) stems

10 mint leaves

1 spring onion (scallion),
  thinly sliced

1 red chilli, thinly sliced

2 tsp light soy sauce

2 tsp crispy fried shallots
  (store-bought or see page 184)

2 pinches of ground black pepper

Here, this Bánh Mì-inspired recipe has another dose of French inspiration by way of using a croissant rather than a classic baguette. This is a weekend breakfast favourite in our house; it's super-easy to throw together. I normally have ingredients like the carrot and daikon pickle pre-prepared and ready in my fridge so I can add a Vietnamese touch to a dish whenever necessary.

Add 1 teaspoon of the oil to a small frying pan and bring to a high heat. Fry the bacon until crisp, then remove and keep warm. Add the remaining oil, then fry the eggs, sunny side up. Remove and keep warm.

Toast the croissants, cut in half and open out on your plate. Spread the pâté on one half and the mayonnaise on the other. Top with the bacon, carrot and daikon pickle and fried eggs.

Stuff in the coriander (cilantro), mint, spring onion (scallion) and chilli, then drizzle over the soy sauce. Sprinkle over the crispy fried shallots and black pepper, and your delicious breakfast is ready.

Prawn Scotch Eggs

Who doesn't love a runny egg yolk, especially when it's covered in delicious meat and then fried? This recipe brings together classic Vietnamese and English snacks, and uses a Chạo Tôm prawn cake to wrap the egg instead of sausagemeat.

MAKES 6

COOKING TIME: 30 MINUTES, PLUS CHILLING

9 large eggs

100g (3½oz) breadcrumbs

Sesame oil, for oiling

1 litre (2 pints) vegetable oil

FOR THE COATING

1kg (2lb 3oz) raw king prawns (shrimp), peeled and deveined

2 lemongrass stalks, finely chopped

1 tsp dried chilli flakes

2 tbsp finely chopped coriander (cilantro) stems and leaves

2 tbsp crushed black peppercorns

4 spring onions (scallions), finely chopped

1 tbsp sugar

1 tsp salt

1 tbsp cornflour (cornstarch)

1 tsp fish sauce

6 tbsp sesame oil

Add all the coating ingredients to a food processor and blitz for 25–30 seconds. Place in the fridge for 3 hours to set, then divide into 6 equal portions.

Meanwhile, boil 6 of the eggs for 6 minutes, remove from the pan and immediately place in iced water for 10 minutes. Peel and set aside.

Beat the remaining 3 eggs in a shallow bowl and place the breadcrumbs in a separate shallow bowl.

Roll the coating pieces into balls then flatten one in the palm of your hand. Place a whole egg in the centre. Wrap the coating around the egg evenly, rubbing a little sesame oil over the outside of the ball to smooth out any lumps and bumps. Repeat with the remaining balls and boiled eggs. Roll all the balls in the beaten egg, then lightly roll in the breadcrumbs to coat all over.

Choose a heavy-based saucepan that is deep enough for the vegetable oil to fill it halfway. Add the oil and bring to 150°C (300°F). An easy way to tell when the oil is ready is by placing a wooden chopstick into the oil and waiting until bubbles start to form around it on the surface of the oil.

Carefully lower in a Scotch egg and deep-fry for 6 minutes, then remove to paper towels to drain and repeat for the remaining eggs.

Vietnamese Pizza

SERVES 1

COOKING TIME: 10 MINUTES

2 sheets of rice paper

5 quail's eggs (or regular eggs),
  separated

50g (1¾oz) mature Gouda, grated

50g (1¾oz) mozzarella, grated

¼ red onion, thinly sliced

1 spring onion (scallion),
  finely chopped

Pinch of crushed black
  peppercorns

Pinch of crispy fried shallots
  (store-bought or see page 184)

1 Thai basil sprig, leaves picked

1 coriander (cilantro) stem, leaves
  picked

Bánh Tráng Nướng is a modern Vietnamese dish made with a rice paper base; it takes just a couple of minutes to cook. On the streets of Vietnam, different vendors create their own versions, even allowing customers to customize their own.

I first spotted a recipe for a Vietnamese pizza online and immediately knew I had to try it for myself. It did not disappoint! I hope you will fall in love on the first bite, just as I did.

Place a sheet of rice paper in a dry frying pan. Pour on half the egg whites and use a spoon to spread them as evenly as you can across the paper, leaving around 2cm (¾in) around the edge. Place a second sheet of rice paper on top and use a spoon to spread the rest of the egg whites across the paper. Place the pan over a medium heat.

Sprinkle over the cheese (I find it easier to add a pinch to weigh down the edges first) and carefully place the yolks evenly across the pizza.

Add the red onion and spring onion (scallion), then cover the pan with a lid for 20 seconds. Remove the lid and cook for a further 45–60 seconds until the cheese has fully melted with a little crust around the edges.

Lift the rice paper to check it is crispy underneath, then add the black pepper, crispy fried shallots and herbs.

Serve this with chilli pepper mayo (see page 179) to spice things up, if you like.

Roast Beef Inside-Out Summer Rolls

MAKES 10

COOKING TIME: 1 HOUR, PLUS CHILLING

500g (1lb 2oz) beef topside (top round)

1 tbsp vegetable oil

1 tsp salt

2 green dessert apples, cut into thin matchsticks

1 yellow (bell) pepper, deseeded and cut into thin matchsticks

1 cucumber, cut into thin matchsticks

20g (¾oz) Thai basil, leaves picked

20g (¾oz) coriander (cilantro) stems, halved

20g (¾oz) mint, leaves picked

2 baby gem lettuce, leaves separated

600ml (20fl oz/2½ cups) pineapple fish sauce (see page 181)

The clue is in the title: what used to be on the inside is now on the outside! This is definitely a dish where you should splash out a little if you can, making sure that the quality of the meat is as high as possible, as it makes a huge difference to the flavour and, importantly, the texture of the rolls.

Preheat the oven to 200°C/400°F/Gas 6.

Dry the meat joint with paper towels, then rub evenly with the oil and salt.

Sear in a dry pan for 2–3 minutes, turning it to sear evenly all over, then put in a roasting tin and cook in the oven for 40–45 minutes. For best results, check the temperature of the meat with a thermometer; you are aiming for 54–60°C (130–140°F) for medium-rare.

Remove from the oven and let the meat rest and cool down to room temperature, then slice the meat into large but super-thin slices. This is to act as your rice paper replacement, so really do go as large as you can and as thin as you can without breaking it.

Fill each slice of beef with the apple, (bell) pepper and cucumber strips, then lay across the Thai basil, coriander (cilantro) and mint. Roll the beef into a cylinder and secure with a wooden toothpick.

Serve with baby gem lettuce and a generous bowl of the pineapple fish sauce dip on the side.

Seafood Patties

MAKES 20

COOKING TIME: 30 MINUTES,
PLUS CHILLING

75ml (5 tbsp) vegetable oil

Pineapple fish sauce or chilli
pepper mayo (see pages 181
and 179), to serve, optional

FOR THE PATTIES

200g (7oz) salmon fillet

200g (7oz) raw king prawns
(shrimp), peeled and deveined

100g (3½oz) crabmeat in brine,
drained

1 tsp salt

2 tsp sugar

1 tsp fish sauce

1 chicken stock cube, crumbled

2 tsp cornflour (cornstarch)

2 tsp ground black pepper

3 spring onions (scallions),
roughly chopped

3 dill stems, roughly chopped

2 tsp lemongrass paste

4 garlic cloves, roughly chopped

Light and moreish, these little patties are a genuine crowd
pleaser; they also freeze really well (defrost in the fridge before
shaping), both before and after cooking. You can make a large
batch, then each time you want to bring them out for a party,
they'll be ready in less than 5 minutes. They are incredibly
versatile, too. Shape them flat and wide for seafood burgers,
or meatball-shaped as appetizers. They also work well as
seafood balls to liven up noodle soups.

Put all the patty ingredients into a food processor and blitz for
8–10 seconds. Make sure not to over-blend as you want nice large
chunks for texture. Refrigerate the mixture for 1–3 hours, taking
out 30 minutes before cooking to bring it to room temperature.
Shape into 20 patties.

Heat 1 teaspoon of oil for each patty in a frying pan and fry the
patties in batches for 2 minutes each side over a medium heat.
Remove the patties and place on paper towels to soak up any
excess oil.

Serve with a dipping sauce of your choice; I like pineapple fish
sauce or chilli pepper mayo.

Smoked Salmon Cucumber Summer Rolls

MAKES 10

PREPARATION TIME: 20 MINUTES

10 sheets summer roll rice paper

200g (7oz) smoked salmon, cut into 10 pieces

1 cucumber, cut into thin matchsticks

1 large carrot, cut into thin matchsticks

1 red (bell) pepper, deseeded and finely cut into thin matchsticks

25g (1oz) coriander (cilantro) stems, halved

25g (1oz) chives, halved

25g (1oz) mint stems, leaves picked

2 baby gem lettuce, leaves separated

FOR THE DIP

60ml (4 tbsp/¼ cup) fish sauce

60ml (4 tbsp/¼ cup) lime juice

60g (2oz) caster (superfine) sugar

2 passion fruit, halved and pulp scooped out

4 garlic cloves, roughly chopped

2 red chillies, roughly chopped

6 rings of canned pineapple

Here is the recipe that your summer party's been missing – the lightest, freshest and tastiest of Vietnamese treats! This is a simple variation on my signature Gỏi Cuốn, Vietnamese Summer Rolls.

Start by making the dip. Add the fish sauce, lime juice and sugar to a small bowl and stir until the sugar has fully dissolved. Add the passion fruit and give it another stir.

In a small food processor, blitz the garlic and chillies for 10–15 seconds until finely minced, then add to the bowl.

Next blitz the pineapple rings for 5–8 seconds to reduce to small chunks; be careful not to purée it. Add to the bowl and mix everything together evenly. Set aside in the fridge to keep fresh and cool.

Half fill a large bowl with lukewarm water. Very quickly dunk your first sheet of rice paper in and then place flat on a chopping board.

Leave the rice paper for 30 seconds to dry a little and then lay a piece of the smoked salmon just below the centre, then lay some of the cucumber, carrot, red (bell) pepper, coriander (cilantro), chives and mint leaves neatly alongside.

To make the rolls, fold the rice paper in like an envelope, bringing the two sides towards the centre over the filling with roughly 3cm (1¼in) folds. Next, fold the top flap down and then roll as tightly as you can from the bottom, all the way up to the top. Repeat with the remaining rice paper and filling.

Serve with a lettuce leaf (you can even use this as a plate) and the dipping sauce.

Steamed Scallops

SERVES 8

COOKING TIME: 20 MINUTES

120g (4oz) mung bean noodles

8 large fresh scallops in the shell
(see note)

5g (⅕oz) fresh ginger, cut into
thin matchsticks

3 spring onions (scallions),
finely chopped

8 coriander (cilantro) stems,
optional

8 tsp crispy fried shallots
(store-bought or see page 184),
optional

40g (1½oz) truffle in oil
(or a drizzle of truffle oil)

FOR THE SAUCE

4 fresh lime leaves, finely sliced
into strips

2 red chillies, minced

4 garlic cloves, minced

4 tbsp light soy sauce

2 tbsp sugar

2 tbsp sesame oil

1 tbsp oyster sauce

The key to the perfect dinner party is to have a knock-out dish that requires minimal effort, yet still blows everyone away. And dishes like this one are the perfect fix – luxurious and naturally flavoursome. Let's get started.

Soak the noodles in hot water for 8–10 minutes until soft, then drain well and set aside.

Put all the sauce ingredients into a small saucepan over a medium heat. When you see bubbles starting to form, take off the heat and set aside.

Remove the scallops and roe from the shell if your fishmonger hasn't already done so, and clean carefully.

Set up your steamer on a high heat and bring to the boiling point. If you don't have a steamer, then take your largest saucepan with a lid, or a small stockpot, and place a bowl upside down on the bottom. Fill the pan with water to just below the top of the bowl, then place a second bowl, the correct way up, securely on top of the first. Put the lid on and you have a working steamer!

Put a small amount of noodles onto each empty shell, then place a scallop with its roe on top, along with a few slices of ginger. Place a single layer of shells in the steamer, close the lid and steam for 4 minutes. Pour a teaspoon of sauce on each scallop, sprinkle the spring onions (scallions) on top and steam for a further minute.

Check the scallops are ready – they will be white with no translucent areas.

Dress each scallop with a stem of coriander (cilantro) and a sprinkle of crispy fried shallots, if using, and a shaving of that oh-so-decadent black truffle to finish (or a drizzle of truffle oil).

NOTE
You can also use frozen, defrosted scallops (without the roe) in place of fresh here, using individual gratin dishes in place of shells.

Tomato Xíu Mại Meatballs

SERVES 4–6

COOKING TIME: 50 MINUTES

2 tbsp vegetable oil

60g (2oz) cornflour (cornstarch)

120ml (4fl oz/½ cup) water

1 spring onion (scallion), greens finely chopped

FOR THE MEATBALLS

500g (1lb 2oz) minced (ground) pork

1 tsp ground black pepper

1 tsp salt

2 tsp sugar

1 tsp garlic paste, or minced garlic

1 tsp lemongrass paste, or minced lemongrass

2 tsp fish sauce

2 large carrots, finely diced

1 large egg

1 x 225g (8oz) can of water chestnuts, drained and finely diced

FOR THE SAUCE

2 garlic cloves, minced

6 firm, ripe tomatoes, diced

2 chicken stock cubes, crumbled

1 tbsp tomato purée (paste)

4 spring onions (scallions), finely chopped

1 red onion, diced

2 tsp sugar

1 tsp salt

This delicious street food dish is traditionally served plain, with a baguette, or taken one step further and used to make amazing Bánh Mì. Alternatively, you can serve on a base of egg noodles, simply with a portion of jasmine rice or even with a fried egg. However you choose to serve them, I'm sure that you're going to love them.

Put all the meatball ingredients into a large bowl and gently mix together with your hands. Once mixed well, shape them into meatballs, about 3–4cm (1¼–1½in) in diameter.

Set up your steamer on a high heat and bring to the boiling point. If you don't have a steamer, then take your largest saucepan with a lid, or a small stockpot, and place a bowl upside down on the bottom. Fill the pan with water to just below the top of the bowl, then place a second bowl, the correct way up, securely on top of the first. Put the lid on and you have a working steamer!

Steam the meatballs for 25–30 minutes.

Put the vegetable oil in a large sauté pan and bring to a medium heat. Add the garlic for the sauce, and toss for 10–15 seconds until browned. Then add the meatballs and cook for 3–4 minutes, turning them to brown evenly. Remove the meatballs from the pan and set aside.

To make the sauce, put the tomatoes in the same pan over a medium heat and cook for 1 minute, then add the remaining sauce ingredients and cook for a further minute.

Mix the cornflour (cornstarch) and water together in a small bowl and pour into the sauce. Add the meatballs and cook for a final 5 minutes. Sprinkle over the spring onion greens and enjoy.

Lemongrass and Ginger Chicken Potato Pie

SERVES 4

COOKING TIME: 1½ HOURS

2 tsp salt

1 litre (34fl oz/4¼ cups) water

1kg (2lb 3oz) potatoes, peeled and diced

100g (3½oz) butter

4 tbsp double (heavy) cream

1 tbsp vegetable oil

500g (1lb 2oz) minced (ground) chicken

2 medium carrots, diced

400ml (14fl oz) coconut cream

120g (4oz) fresh shiitake mushrooms

2 medium onions, diced

3 spring onions (scallions), finely chopped

10g (⅓oz) dill, finely chopped

180g (6½oz) Cheddar cheese, grated

FOR THE SAUCE

2 tbsp sesame oil

2 chicken stock cubes, crumbled

1 tsp chilli paste

1 tsp garlic paste

1 tsp lemongrass paste

1 tsp ginger paste

1 tsp ground turmeric

1 tsp paprika

3 tsp sugar

2 tsp dark soy sauce

1 tsp fish sauce

1 tsp rice wine vinegar

100ml (3½fl oz) water

I love lemongrass chicken; I have so many different recipes for dishes using it and am always ready to add a new one to the list. This type of pie is not traditionally Vietnamese, but here I've brought in some classic flavours and paired them with potatoes. Instead of dairy, I prefer using coconut cream as it gives a wonderful richness to the meal and brings all the different flavours together perfectly. This now guarantees a happy dinner table at our house and hopefully it will prove to be the same at yours.

Add all the sauce ingredients to a small bowl and mix together.

Add the salt and water to a large pan and bring to the boil. Add the potatoes and cook for 10–15 minutes until soft, then drain, put into a bowl and add the butter and cream. Mash until smooth, then set aside.

Heat the oil in a medium pan, add the chicken and carrots and cook, stirring, for 2–3 minutes. Pour on the sauce and cook for a further 2–3 minutes, ensuring the meat is coated evenly. Add the coconut cream, cover with a lid and simmer for 20 minutes.

Preheat the oven to 180°C/350°F/Gas 4.

Add the mushrooms, onions, spring onions (scallions) and dill to the chicken and stir well. Tip into a baking dish, spread the mashed potato on top, sprinkle over the grated cheese and bake for 30 minutes until golden.

SWEET TREATS

Room for Dessert

Many times it has been pointed out to me that my eyes are bigger than my belly. And just as many times I have then set about proving them wrong. I am on occasion one of those annoying people who, despite being full to bursting point, will happily tell the waiter that I have a little spare room in my stomach for dessert. However, this is only ever for a berry crumble, a cheesecake, a treacle sponge pudding, or another sweet Western-style dessert. Vietnamese desserts simply aren't eaten in this way.

European/American and Vietnamese desserts are fundamentally different dishes. For most of my life I have considered them as entirely unrelated entities.

Traditional Vietnamese desserts are both sweet and savoury, which is probably why I love them so much and will often enjoy at home for lunch or occasionally even dinner. They are generally made from rice and will always have a salty note to them.

In Vietnam, cakes and desserts represent a simple celebration of gratitude. They would always accompany a celebration like a wedding or Tết (Vietnamese New Year). Outside of specific festivities like these you would most likely only eat them as a treat at a street market. As a child I would always jump at the chance to go to the market with mum, my aunties or grandma, mainly in the hope of getting one of these treats. I especially loved going to the night market, as the chances were much higher! Being from a rural part of Vietnam, our day was very much determined by the sun, and everyone would generally get up and go to bed in sync with it. So, the night market always felt like a special treat on those rare occasions I was allowed to go. Just the simple addition of lights hanging from the same stalls that would be selling fruit and vegetables during the day was enough to fill my young eyes with wonder. Our village night market was humble by any standards, but just having a place to meet where you could share stories and jokes while enjoying a dessert and perhaps a sweet milk tea really helped to bring the community together. I still cherish my memories of those evenings, and even now, certain desserts can transport me back in time to those stalls.

This chapter includes some of those Vietnamese desserts, but with a twist. My aim is to combine my experience of both Vietnamese and British desserts, while stripping away the complexity of Vietnamese layering and the precision of the British bake. Instead, the focus is on simple flavour combinations that are uncomplicated to create, yet delicious, and perfect after a large meal, or served with a tea, as you would enjoy them at a traditional night market.

Hanoi-style Egg Coffee

SERVES 1

PREPARATION TIME: 10 MINUTES

2 large egg yolks

½ tsp vanilla extract

20ml (1 tbsp plus 1 tsp) condensed milk

40ml (2 tbsp plus 2 tsp) freshly made filtered coffee

Pinch of cocoa powder

Pinch of desiccated (dried shredded) coconut

Vietnam is the world's second largest coffee producer, mainly Robusta beans, which tend to be used for instant and low-grade coffee; but, with their lower acidity and deeper bitter flavour, Robusta beans are making a comeback and are far more valued these days. Coffee drinking has major cultural significance in Vietnam, and Viet-style drip coffee is now being served all over the world.

This recipe is for a variation that leans more towards dessert than a typical morning espresso. Egg coffee, or Cà Phê Trứng, was invented in Hanoi in the 1940s but has had a resurgence recently due to its popularity on social media. The good news is that it doesn't just look good, it tastes amazing too.

Put the egg yolks, vanilla extract and condensed milk into a small bowl and whisk for 5 minutes until smooth and a little frothy.

Pour the mixture into a glass mug, then slowly pour the hot coffee directly on top, aiming for the centre when pouring, so the foam stays intact.

Leave for a few seconds for the coffee to settle, then sprinkle a little cocoa powder and coconut on the top to finish.

Banana Tapioca Cake with Coconut Custard

SERVES 12

COOKING TIME: 30 MINUTES, PLUS COOLING

1kg (2lb 3oz) bananas, peeled and sliced into diagonal discs about 5mm (¼in) thick

70g (2½oz) brown sugar

½ tsp salt

180g (6½oz) tapioca starch

½ tsp ground turmeric

75ml (5 tbsp) water

2 tsp vegetable oil

6 Cadbury Flake bars (or similar), broken into crumbs

150g (5oz) roasted pistachios, roughly crushed in a pestle and mortar

FOR THE COCONUT CUSTARD

400ml (14fl oz) coconut cream

½ tsp salt

1 tbsp sugar

1 tsp cornflour (cornstarch)

2 spring onions (scallions), green parts only, finely chopped

The textures and flavours of this cake perfectly encapsulate Vietnamese desserts! It's sweet yet savoury, soft yet bouncy and chewy. Having taken my nieces and nephew to many ice-cream parlours over the past decade, I have ordered my fair share of banana and chocolate desserts. Whilst chocolate is not a common ingredient in Vietnam, it works well here as the perfect twist to an otherwise classic dessert.

Place almost all of the banana pieces in a bowl (reserve and set aside about 1 banana's worth of pieces) with the brown sugar and salt and mix together gently so as not to break the pieces. Add the tapioca starch, turmeric and water, and continue to mix gently until it's an even golden yellow colour throughout. Set aside.

Set up your steamer on a high heat and bring to the boiling point. If you don't have a steamer, then take your largest saucepan with a lid, or a small stockpot, and place a bowl upside down on the bottom. Fill the pan with water to just below the top of the bowl, then place a second bowl, the correct way up, securely on top of the first. Put the lid on and you have a working steamer!

Place a 20cm (8in) cake tin (pan), ideally springform, in the steamer to warm up for 2 minutes. Take out and lightly grease using the vegetable oil.

Pour in the banana mixture, placing the reserved banana pieces on top, and steam on a high heat for 20 minutes. Check to see if the cake is ready by poking the centre with a toothpick; if it comes out clean, then it's ready. Remove from the steamer and leave to cool down for 30 minutes before serving.

For the coconut custard, pour the coconut cream into a small saucepan and bring up to a medium heat. Add the salt, sugar, cornflour (cornstarch) and spring onions (scallions) and stir slowly until all the lumps are gone.

Serve a slice of banana cake, pour over the hot coconut custard, then generously sprinkle with chocolate crumbs and pistachios.

Chilli and Lemongrass Spiced Pears

A poached pear: simple, delicious and a perfect vessel to carry the flavours of Vietnam. This elegantly uncomplicated dessert was a much-loved part of our autumn menu at The Little Viet Kitchen.

SERVES 4

COOKING TIME: 40 MINUTES, PLUS COOLING

4 firm Rocha pears (or use Williams or Comice)

500g (1lb 2oz) sugar

2 lemongrass stalks, crushed

4 star anise

2 cinnamon sticks

2 red chillies

2 fresh lime leaves

5g (⅕oz) fresh ginger, crushed

Zest of ½ lemon, pared using a swivel peeler

TO SERVE

200ml (7fl oz) coconut cream

40g (1½oz) honey-roasted cashew nuts, roughly crushed in a pestle and mortar

Peel the pears and slice the bottoms off so that they stand upright, leaving the stems intact.

Choose a saucepan so that when the water is added it will sit about halfway up the height of the pears. Cut a round piece of baking parchment to fit inside the pan, snip a 3cm (1¼in) diameter hole in the middle and set aside.

Put 1.5 litres (50fl oz/3¼ pints) water into the saucepan and bring to the boil. Add the remaining ingredients except for the pears and stir until the sugar dissolves. Turn the heat down to a simmer, then add the pears, standing upright.

Place the parchment disc on top of the pears to make sure they are fully submerged and leave to simmer for 25–30 minutes, depending on the size of the pears.

Take off the heat and leave the pears to cool down in the juice. Don't worry if it takes a while; the longer you leave it, the more the pears will absorb those spices.

Serve with a dollop of coconut cream, a drizzle of the juice and a sprinkle of roasted cashew nuts.

Coconut Panna Cotta with a Lemongrass Peach Coulis

SERVES 4

COOKING TIME: 20 MINUTES, PLUS CHILLING

FOR THE PANNA COTTA

1 tsp vegetable oil

300ml (10fl oz/1¼ cups) double (heavy) cream

1 x 12g (½oz) sachet of gelatine powder

250ml (8fl oz/1 cup) coconut cream

1 tsp vanilla extract

50g (2oz) caster (superfine) sugar

FOR THE PEACHES

3 ripe peaches, pitted and cubed (or use 450g/1lb frozen chunks)

2 lemongrass stalks, crushed

1 red chilli, halved

Juice of 2 limes

120g (4oz) caster (superfine) sugar

TO SERVE

6g (⅕oz) dried raspberries

6g (⅕oz) flaked (slivered) almonds

4 mint stems, leaves picked (optional)

This is my Vietnamese twist on one of my favourite Italian desserts. Light and creamy, a panna cotta is the perfect end to a big meal and always helps finish the evening with a smile. This recipe is a nod to my time in Italy and the many friends I made there, who will always hold a special place in my heart as they encouraged me to take the leap into working in food, and follow my dream.

Using the vegetable oil, lightly grease 4 ramekin dishes and set aside.

Put the cream and gelatine into a small saucepan over a medium heat, and stir together. Bring to a simmer and add the coconut cream, vanilla extract and sugar. Stir continuously until the gelatine has completely dissolved, being careful not to let it boil at any point. Remove from the heat and strain through a sieve (strainer) into a jug (pitcher).

Pour evenly into your greased ramekins and place in the fridge for 3–4 hours to set.

Meanwhile, put the peaches, lemongrass, chilli, lime juice, 100ml (3½fl oz) water and the sugar into a small saucepan over a medium heat and simmer for 15 minutes, stirring often to ensure it doesn't burn. Take off the heat and leave to cool for 10 minutes.

RECIPE CONTINUES

Remove and discard the lemongrass and chilli, then remove half the peaches and set aside.

Blitz the remaining mixture in a food processor or blender for 5–10 seconds until smooth. Try the coulis at this point and adjust to your taste, adding more sugar to sweeten or lime juice to sour, then blend for a few more seconds if needed, before passing the coulis through a sieve and putting in the fridge to cool.

To serve, dip the ramekin bases into just-boiled water for 3 seconds, to release the panna cottas, and turn out onto your serving plates. Pour over the coulis and top with the reserved poached peaches. Lastly, sprinkle over the raspberries and flaked (slivered) almonds, and garnish with the mint leaves if using.

Avocado and Berries with Condensed Milk

SERVES 2

PREPARATION TIME: 10 MINUTES

2 ripe avocados

4 tbsp whole milk

10 raspberries

8 strawberries

4 tbsp condensed milk, or more to taste

6 mint leaves

5g (⅕oz) roasted shelled pistachios, roughly crushed in a pestle and mortar

Having loved this my entire life, I may be a little biased, but I believe that this will be the easiest dessert you'll ever make, and one of the tastiest!

Avocado is used to make a very popular Vietnamese smoothie of avocado and milk blitzed with crushed ice, then drizzled with condensed milk. It is also often eaten raw with a little sugar sprinkled on top.

This simple dessert is essentially a combination of those two classic Vietnamese treats, but with fresh berries on top to cut through the sweetness.

Halve the avocados and remove the stones and skin. Place the flesh into a bowl and use a fork to break into small lumps. Add the whole milk, continuing to mix but keeping the texture rough with plenty of chunks.

Spoon onto small dessert plates, then place the berries on top and drizzle over the condensed milk. Adjust the amount of condensed milk to your taste; the more you add, the sweeter it will be.

Top with the mint leaves and crushed pistachios.

SAUCES & EXTRAS

The recipes in this chapter are extremely versatile and will perfectly complement many of the recipes in this book. Personally, my larder always has a stock of them, as I find them invaluable to my everyday cooking and, as well as the recipes in this book, I use them in a whole variety of dishes, Vietnamese or otherwise. They each help to elevate a dish, adding a delicious flavour and freshness to almost anything. You can, of course, use store-bought equivalents for some of these, but I believe a homemade version crafted with love and fresh ingredients will help to take any dish to a whole other level.

Spring Onion Oil

MAKES 300ML (10FL OZ/1¼ CUPS)

COOKING TIME: 10 MINUTES

120ml (4fl oz/½ cup) vegetable oil
25g (1oz) red shallots, finely chopped
200g (7oz) spring onions (scallions), finely chopped
1 tbsp light soy sauce

Add the vegetable oil to a small pan over a medium heat. Once hot, add the shallots and spring onions (scallions), cook for 30 seconds, then take off the heat immediately.

Add the soy sauce, stir together and leave to cool.

Store in an airtight container for up to 3 months in the fridge.

Chilli Pepper Mayo

MAKES 165ML (5½FL OZ)

PREPARATION TIME: 5 MINUTES

120ml (4fl oz/½ cup) mayonnaise
30ml (2 tbsp) sweet chilli sauce
15ml (1 tbsp) sriracha chilli sauce
15g (½oz) ground black pepper

Put all the ingredients into a bowl and mix together well.

This will store, covered, for up to 2 days in the fridge.

Lemongrass Chilli Oil

MAKES 900ML (30FL OZ/3¾ CUPS)

COOKING TIME: 40 MINUTES

500ml (17fl oz/generous 2 cups) vegetable oil

25g (1oz) garlic, minced

50g (1¾oz) red shallots, minced

100g (3½oz) lemongrass, minced

25g (1oz) dried chilli flakes

50g (1¾oz) caster (superfine) sugar

15g (½oz) salt

15ml (1 tbsp) fish sauce

15ml (1 tbsp) light soy sauce

200ml (7fl oz) chilli oil

Add the vegetable oil to a small pan over a medium heat. Once hot, add the garlic and shallots and cook for 2 minutes until the garlic starts to turn golden.

Add the remaining ingredients, reduce the heat to the lowest setting and simmer for a further 30 minutes, stirring occasionally to avoid the sugar burning.

Take off the heat and leave to cool overnight, uncovered to ensure it has air flow.

Store in an airtight container for up to 3 months in the fridge.

Carrot and Daikon Pickle

MAKES A 1-LITRE (34FL OZ/GENEROUS 4 CUPS) JAR

COOKING TIME: 10 MINUTES, PLUS COOLING

500ml (17fl oz/generous 2 cups) rice vinegar

500g (1lb 2oz) caster (superfine) sugar

250g (9oz) carrots, cut into thin matchsticks

250g (9oz) daikon/mooli (or you can use radishes), cut into thin matchsticks

Heat up the rice vinegar and sugar in a saucepan to about 80–85°C (176–185°F), stirring until all the sugar has dissolved. Take off the heat and leave to cool completely.

Put the carrots and daikon into a clean, sterilized jar (run it through the dishwasher, with no detergent) and pour over the cooled vinegar. It can be eaten after 3 hours but is better if left overnight.

Store in an airtight jar for up to 2 weeks in the fridge.

Tamarind
Fish Sauce

MAKES 340ML (11½FL OZ)

PREPARATION TIME: 10 MINUTES

50ml (3½ tbsp) tamarind paste

10ml (2 tsp) lime juice

50ml (3½ tbsp) fish sauce

130ml (4½fl oz) sweet chilli sauce

100ml (3½fl oz) water

15g (½oz) garlic, minced

25g (1oz) red chillies, minced

Put all the ingredients into a bowl and mix together well.

Store, covered, for up to 5 days in the fridge.

Pineapple
Fish Sauce

MAKES 200ML (7FL OZ)

COOKING TIME: 15 MINUTES

50ml (3½ tbsp) fish sauce

100ml (3½fl oz) water

120g (4oz) caster (superfine) sugar

50ml (3½ tbsp) lime juice

15g (½oz) garlic, minced

25g (1oz) red chillies, minced

50g (1¾oz) fresh (or use canned) pineapple, minced

Put the fish sauce, water, sugar and lime juice into a small saucepan and bring to the boil over a medium heat. Remove any impurities from the top of the sauce, if there are any, then take off the heat immediately and leave to cool.

When completely cool, add the garlic, chillies and pineapple and mix well; they should float to the top. Pour into an airtight bottle or jar with a lid.

Store, covered, for up to 5 days in the fridge.

Nước Chấm Fish Sauce

MAKES 200ML (7FL OZ)

COOKING TIME: 15 MINUTES

50ml (3½ tbsp) fish sauce

100ml (3½fl oz) water

120g (4oz) caster (superfine) sugar

50ml (3½ tbsp) lime juice

15g (½oz) garlic, minced

25g (1oz) red chillies, minced

Put the fish sauce, water, sugar and lime juice into a small saucepan and bring to the boil over a medium heat. Remove any impurities from the top of the sauce, if there are any, then take off the heat immediately and leave to cool.

When completely cool, add the garlic and chillies and mix well; they should float to the top. Pour into an airtight bottle or jar with a lid.

Store, covered, for up to 5 days in the fridge.

Ginger Fish Sauce

MAKES 340ML (11½FL OZ)

PREPARATION TIME: 10 MINUTES

60ml (4 tbsp/¼ cup) lime juice

50ml (3½ tbsp) fish sauce

130ml (4½fl oz) sweet chilli sauce

100ml (3½fl oz) water

15g (½oz) garlic, minced

25g (1oz) red chillies, minced

25g (1oz) fresh ginger, minced

Put all the ingredients into a bowl and mix together well. Pour into an airtight bottle or jar with a lid.

Store, covered, for up to 5 days in the fridge.

Chilli and Garlic Soy Sauce

MAKES 200ML (7FL OZ)

COOKING TIME: 15 MINUTES

50ml (3½ tbsp) light soy sauce

100ml (3½fl oz) water

120g (4oz) caster (superfine) sugar

50ml (3½ tbsp) lime juice

15g (½oz) garlic, minced

25g (1oz) red chillies, minced

Put the soy sauce, water, sugar and lime juice into a small saucepan and bring to the boil over a medium heat. As soon as it boils, take off the heat and leave to cool.

When completely cool, add the garlic and chillies and mix well; they should float to the top. Pour into an airtight bottle or jar with a lid.

Store, covered, for up to 5 days in the fridge.

Crispy Fried Shallots

This is to make a large batch to keep in your larder. You will be using these a lot in this book, and soon on pretty much everything else too!

MAKES 1KG (2LB 3OZ)

COOKING TIME: 40 MINUTES

1kg (2lb 3oz) red shallots

1 litre (34fl oz/4¼ cups) vegetable oil

Peel the shallots and chop as finely as you can.

Heat the oil in a wok on the lowest setting for around 5–7 minutes. An easy way to tell when the oil is ready is by placing a wooden chopstick into the oil and waiting until bubbles start to form around it on the surface of the oil.

Carefully add half the shallots to the hot oil and deep-fry for 10–12 minutes until golden brown. Remove with a mesh strainer onto sheets of paper towel, making sure they are in a single layer so they stay crisp, and repeat with the remaining shallots. Leave overnight to dry.

Put the crispy shallots into an airtight jar once completely dry and store for up to 6 months at room temperature.

Index

About the author

Thuy Diem Pham is an author and chef, and owner of the multi-award winning London restaurant The Little Viet Kitchen. Having moved to the UK aged seven, Thuy's distinctive approach to cooking combines her genuine understanding of Vietnamese culture and cuisine, with a deft handle on London's food scene; she's widely regarded as one of the UK's most prominent voices on Vietnamese cuisine.

Acknowledgements

If I have learned anything over the past year while writing this book, it is that I am blessed. Despite it being one of the toughest to date, I wouldn't have it any other way. I'm so grateful for my family, who are always there holding an umbrella when it's raining and a net when I fall. Also, to friends old and new, thank you for all the moments of joy you bring to my life when most needed, even if it's just a terrible joke or two.

A special thank you to my husband, for back-to-back daddy day care throughout the creation of this book. Even the best job in the world has its hard moments, although not many, as he is a perfect little angel, obviously. Thank you for never stopping believing in me, even when I question myself.

Elly, thank you. You have been the calm to my fire, and your positive perspective and patience through this whole process has been thoroughly appreciated.

A huge thank you to HexClad for your ingenious cookware, not only is it perfect for Vietnamese cuisine, but the quality is like being in a professional kitchen, whilst at home. Thank you to Gozney, for the pizza oven of my dreams. My Bánh Tráng Nướng (Vietnamese pizza) was cooked to perfection! Kamado Joe UK, for providing me with what is quite simply the best BBQ grill ever! It made recipe-testing way more fun; it genuinely is a game-changer and I'm hooked! Thank you, Chef's Locker, for making sure my ingredients are always chopped to perfection with your incredible Japanese knives. I adore them! And finally to Waitrose, reliably well stocked with some of the most consistently good produce in the UK. Thank you for continuing to add South East Asian ingredients to your shelves, helping me to introduce Vietnamese cooking with ease to my friends and customers alike.

This book has come to life in the most natural and organic way. An unexpected direction for me, but it just felt right and now seems like it was always meant to be my next step. I found comfort while writing it, as it allowed me to fully embrace the changes and new challenges in my life. To be able to share it in this way is an honour and a privilege and I am so grateful to Quadrille for giving me the support and allowing me the freedom to walk this new path.

Georgina Hayden, your love and generosity continue to inspire me. Not only are you an incredibly talented chef and author but you never fail to amaze me by making the juggle of motherhood and career look far easier than we all know it to be! Thank you for being my guiding angel. Thank you for illuminating my cookbook world.

Thanks so much to the stars that are Laura, Joss, Tabitha, El and Alicia – the shoot was an unforgettable experience in the best possible sense. It has been a pleasure and so inspiring to work with such an accomplished and talented team at the absolute top of their game.

Stacey, thank you for welcoming me into and making me feel so at home in the Quadrille family. Your kindness goes a long way, but your knowledgeable hand on the tiller has been invaluable in bringing this book to life, and I can't thank you enough.

Last but not least, to you! If you have enjoyed reading and tasting the recipes in my book, I am truly grateful for your love and support. My journey has been far more exciting having you cooking and eating alongside me! I hope you have enjoyed trying these recipes as much as I did creating them.

Love and gratitude always,

Thuy xxx

Publishing Director Sarah Lavelle

Commissioning Editor Stacey Cleworth

Head of Design Claire Rochford

Designer Alicia House

Photographer Laura Edwards

Photographer Assistants Matthew Hague and Jo Cowan

Food Stylist Joss Herd

Food Stylist Assistant El Kemp

Prop Stylist Tabitha Hawkins

Cover illustration Jordan Amy Lee

Head of Production Stephen Lang

Senior Production Controller Katie Jarvis

First published in 2023 by Quadrille,
an imprint of Hardie Grant Publishing

Quadrille
52–54 Southwark Street
London SE1 1UN
quadrille.com

Cataloguing in Publication Data: a catalogue record for this book is available from the British Library.

9781787139688